101 Ways to Love

101 Ways to Love Your Job

Sarah Urquhart

Published by

THE
COACHING ACADEMY

0800 783 4823

Copyright ' 2003 Sarah Urquhart and The Coaching Academy UK Ltd.
All rights reserved. No part of this publication may be reproduced, stored in
a retrieval system, or transmitted in any form or by any means, electronic,
mechanical, photocopying, recording or otherwise without the prior
permission of the publishers.

First published in Great Britain in 2003 by
The Coaching Academy UK Ltd.
Academy House
20 Landport Terrace
Portsmouth
Hampshire PO1 2RG
Tel: 0800 783 4823
Fax: 023 9286 1584
Email: info@topcoachingschool.com
Web: www.topcoachingschool.com

Edited by Colin C. Edwards
Cover Design by Designline Graphics, Havant, Hampshire.
Typeset by ALS Designs, Portsmouth, Hampshire. Tel: 023 9283 1023

Printed and bound in Great Britain by
PPG Design & Print Ltd, Portsmouth, Hampshire. Tel: 023 9266 2232

This book is sold subject to the condition that it shall not, by way of trade or
otherwise, be lent, resold, hired out or otherwise circulated without the
publisher s prior consent in any form of binding or cover other than that in
which it is published and without a similar condition including this
condition being imposed upon the subsequent purchaser.

British Library Cataloguing in Publication Data.
ISBN 0-9539073-0-9

ACKNOWLEDGEMENTS

I would like to thank The Portsmouth Evening News for giving me permission to reproduce extracts from my Careers Clinic articles, which I have written for them over the past 3 years.

I would also like to thank Jonathan Jay, Founder and Managing Director of The Coaching Academy for inviting me to pull together all of these articles to form my hints and tips for anyone wishing to be happier and more fulfilled in their working lives. And of course, thanks to Colin Edwards, my editor.

Finally, I would like to thank all my clients and all those anonymous people whose conversations I have overheard who have given me inspiration for many of these articles.

Sarah Urquhart

INTRODUCTION

WELCOME TO 101 WAYS TO LOVE YOUR JOB.

Yes, it really is possible to love your job. Just spending a few minutes with this book on a regular basis and then applying the tips it contains will improve your life. You can repeat the dose as often as you like.

There are several books that explain the techniques and methods behind the fast-growing popularity of coaching. This one is different!

Sarah Urquhart takes real life situations, usually from an office environment, turns them into brief questions and then provides answers to provoke effective actions. Her solutions are punchy, positive, practical and pragmatic.

The book presents many of the weekly articles that were originally written for the Saturday editions of Portsmouth Evening News. Under the 'Careers Clinic' banner, they have an emphasis on successful job hunting, career changes and happiness at work.

You may be happy at work, you may run your own business, you may even be enjoying time out from work even so, each page contains valuable self-discovery insights and hints that can still help everyone to create an even happier and better balanced lifestyle, both at work and at leisure.

Turn to the page that refers to your present concerns or, just dip into the book at random. Either way, each minute that you spend with an open mind will suggest positive changes that you can introduce right now.

Do not be deceived by the simplicity of these pages. Complications can only impede progress and it is often within the simplest of concepts that great discoveries are made.

Happy reading!

Jonathan Jay
Founder and Managing Director of The Coaching Academy

ACHIEVING

The secret to achieving whatever you want in life — whether it is a better paid job, a bigger house or your ideal partner — is to set goals. To consistently achieve what you want takes more than hope; it takes planning.

Firstly, you have to identify what it is that you want. You can decide what you want and then work out a plan of action of how to achieve it — you do not have to accept what other people say that you should be satisfied with. If you have difficulty in deciding what you want, think about what you do not want — that is often easier. Chances are that you want the opposite of what you say you do not want!

So now you have decided what you want to achieve, for example a better-paid job, you must set yourself a deadline for reaching this goal (say, for example, three months from today).

The next part of goal setting is to identify your current situation in relation to this goal. Make a note of all the things you have tried so far to achieve it. Also, write down all the facts that you know. For example, job advertisements showing that other companies pay more than you currently earn.

Next, you need to brainstorm all the possible things that you could do in order to achieve your goal. You could consider obtaining more qualifications or asking your boss for a pay rise. At this stage, imagine that there are no obstacles such as a lack of money or time.

Finally, decide which of the options you would commit to doing — which ones appeal to you most? Then you must plan when you will take action on these options. It is a good idea to do this exercise with a friend so that you can motivate each other to take the necessary action.

ADRENALINE

Stress — we all need a bit of it to motivate us. Too much stress however, affects your relationships, your effectiveness at work and your health.

Stress has always been here. When we hunted with spears, the 'fight or flight' response kept us safe when we were faced with a sabre-toothed tiger. These days, our sabre-toothed tigers often take the form of our bosses or our partners and it is no longer appropriate to flee or fight. Even so, we still experience all the appropriate physical symptoms, including increased adrenaline. If we allow these physical symptoms to build up on top of each other, we eventually experience loss of effective performance and even suffer illness.

So what can you do? There are two ways to tackle stress. One is by working on the effects of stress. This includes incorporating some form of relaxation every day such as exercise or meditation.

The other way of tackling stress is by working on the cause of stress. What makes you stressed? What can you do to reduce this? For example if your workload causes you stress, you might consider attending a time management course or re-negotiating your workload with your boss.

AGE

Getting older is something we cannot get away from. Unfortunately there will always be employers who discriminate against age — they will either claim you are too young or too old. If you, or an employer, believe age is a barrier to success, it will be. Using age as an excuse is a limiting belief that you can overcome.

Older performers like Dame Judi Dench, Trevor MacDonald and Michael Parkinson have refused to let their age stop them from holding desirable jobs. In fact, they seem to be more in demand than ever.

The last National Census showed that there are more people over 60 than there are under 16. There will be more need for older workers in the future. In addition, the Government is talking about the possibility of extending the official retirement age, so there will be more and more encouragement for older workers to be employed.

With maturity, we become more confident in our own ability and need less supervision than younger workers. We know what we want to achieve in our lives and are much more stable in our relationships.

However, it is also important to keep up-to-date at work and in your industry and to renew your skills and knowledge regularly. You can do this by reading trade magazines and going on training courses. When you show that you maintain energy and enthusiasm in your work then your age becomes less of an issue for all concerned.

ANGER

Stabbings in schools, Road Rage, shouting at your colleagues/kids/dog — these are all examples of anger being expressed after levels of suppression have escalated things past your tolerance level.

Outbursts of anger are at the furthest end of an emotional response spectrum. Anger outbursts are a form of fight response — at the other end of the spectrum is the flight response. Along the way, before an outburst, are internal dialogue, irritation, negative feelings, non-assertiveness and inaction. All of which, if left unchecked, will eventually end in the fight end of the spectrum being activated. Outbursts of anger indicate that you have been ignoring the warning signs along the way.

Some people who regularly display this kind of behaviour report/believe that they feel better after an outburst. Medical research actually shows different — we produce some negative chemical reactions in our bodies when we frequently push ourselves to our emotional limits and this can be detrimental to our long-term health.

It s also very difficult for colleagues and loved ones to know how to behave around a person who reacts with angry outbursts — most people want to maintain harmony and will therefore modify their behaviour to attempt to avoid angry situations — so although you might feel better, it s unlikely that anyone else around you does!

If you re reading this and thinking that this doesn t apply to you — are you being complete honest? Monitor your behaviour for a week — or if you re feeling brave, ask someone else to monitor your behaviour — and notice exactly how many times you do choose the fight response. You might be surprised.

ASKING

Recent British and European draft legislation enables employees to ask for more flexible working arrangements so that they can balance their home and work commitments. Whilst these laws cannot guarantee that your requests will be granted, the way that you approach your request will significantly influence the results that you achieve.

The secret to successful asking is to prepare beforehand. Firstly, decide exactly what you do want. Also, decide where you can be flexible and where you absolutely cannot negotiate. Then think about the situation from the other person s point of view. What is likely to be important to them? What objections might they have to your request? How can you reassure them that their worries are groundless?

Book a meeting with the right person, the one who has the authority to negotiate with you. Tell them in advance what you want to discuss, so that they have time to prepare. It might even help to put your reason for the meeting in writing. You may think that giving them forewarning of your request will ensure a negative reply. However, people frequently reject requests because they have been taken by surprise.

When you have the meeting, be prepared to listen to the other person s views and concerns, as well as explaining your own requirements to them. If you appear flexible and willing to negotiate, that will stand you in good stead for finding a solution that suits you both.

During the meeting, keep your outcome in mind. Be courageous enough to continue the meeting until you reach a solution that you are both happy with. This assertive negotiation will benefit you both, and improve your relationship.

Be careful what you ask for. When you ask for what you want, with a confident expectation of success, then as long as you have done your preparation well, you will probably get it!

ASSERTIVENESS

Being assertive is not necessarily easy. For many people of naturally quiet disposition, it can be a daunting prospect. It takes courage to stand up for what you want whilst also respecting the other person s wants and needs. So, what is the difference between assertiveness and aggression? Assertive people state their opinions or wants calmly and firmly. Aggressive people give orders and possibly shout or use bullying tactics.

So how can you tell whether you are being assertive, aggressive or submissive in your dealings with peers, subordinates or superiors?

Assertive people believe that their opinions are important but they also listen to, and acknowledge, the opinions of others. Aggressive people refuse to listen to alternative points of view and attempt to manipulate others into doing what they want. Submissive people do not discuss their wants and needs and typically agree to things when they do not want to.

Think about how you behave in certain circumstances — are you assertive in some situations but not others? In today s busy world, it is sometimes easier to behave aggressively in order to get things done quickly, but think about the long-term impact that you may be having on a relationship. Assertive people aim for all parties to win when they are dealing with others. Aggressiveness and submission always result in someone winning and someone losing and that is bad for sound long-term relationships.

Behaving assertively takes practice and sometimes the payoffs are not immediate. However, if you are consistently assertive then people that you deal with will learn to treat you fairly and will know that you can be relied upon to be equally fair in return. As a result, you will gain their respect and a willingness to work along with you.

BALANCE

It is vitally important to get the balance of our lives right to reduce stress and increase enjoyment. We frequently hear stories of people who have 'downsized' to get a better quality of life. So how can you achieve balance in your life, even if a total change is not an option or does not appeal to you?

Firstly, write down the areas of your life that are important to you. These could include things like; career, money, relationships, health, exercise, personal development, spirituality, relaxation and so on.

Now draw a circle on a sheet of paper. Imagine that the categories you wrote down are spokes of a wheel, so draw the appropriate number of spokes within the circle. Next, for each spoke, shade in how much time you currently spend on the different areas. This should give you the shape of a wheel within your circle — is your wheel fairly round or would you have a bumpy ride if you put in on a bike?

The ideal wheel is perfectly round, with equal quality time spent on each area of your life that you consider to be important. So, if your wheel is a bit uneven, how do you find the time to fit in all these other things? Be completely honest and analyse your day to see if you have fallen into any bad habits. Do you stay at the office longer because you choose to rather than because you have to? Do you watch hours of television — even if the programme does not really interest you? You can 'steal' this wasted time back, to spend on doing things that will really improve your balance.

Now, think about what you love doing but that you do not often allow yourself the time or money for. Right here and now, commit to doing this once a week for the next four weeks. You will find that giving more time to yourself makes you feel more inclined to give to others and you will already feel more balanced. Keep a regular check on the spokes of your wheel to make sure it stays as round as possible.

If you struggle to power your life forward with a seriously out of balance wheel, you must not be surprised if it falls off!

BEING

Many goal setting techniques and procedures focus on what you want to have and do.

It is worth remembering that we are human beings, not 'human doings' or 'human havings'.

When you focus on who you want to be, the 'have' and 'do' benefits tend to happen anyway.

Take a few minutes to make a list of how you would like to be. Do not just consider the things like 'be richer' or 'be thinner'. Think about your emotions and feelings too. For example, 'be more successful, happier, a nicer person, a better parent or partner, more confident'.

Once you have your list you will know what qualities, feelings and 'beings' are really important to you. Now work through your list and define how you will recognise these qualities when you have them. How will you know that you are more confident? How will it feel to be more confident? How will you act differently then? How will your attitude to others change?

Answering these questions for each item on your list will create a blueprint of your behaviour in order to help you feel the way you want to be all of the time. Do not beat yourself up if it takes a while to achieve all that you want to be. Everything that is worthwhile in life takes time.

Ask yourself why you want to be different. Let the anticipation of the benefits keep you on track and do not be surprised when your 'do' and 'have' desires also materialise in your life.

BELIEFS

We all have beliefs that we have learned from our family or experiences. As we grow older, we discard some beliefs that we used to have, as they are no longer useful to us. However, we also keep hold of many beliefs — some of which are helpful, such as 'I have got a good memory', but also ones that are unhelpful in our adult life, such as 'It is rude to say no'.

You may think that it is not too important what you believe. You are wrong. Our beliefs become the 'rules' by which we live.

Think about some of the beliefs you may have. You can identify them by answering the following questions; 'life is ?, I am ?,' etc. Write a few down and examine them. Do any of them stop you doing things you would like to do? Are any out of date, just like your childhood belief in Father Christmas? Are they your beliefs or did you borrow any that you would like to get rid of now?

For the beliefs that you would like to get rid of, imagine yourself in the future if you continue with them. What will you miss out on? What wouldn t you have done? Does it feel good or bad to have missed out?

Next, think about a positive belief you would like to have instead. Imagine yourself in the future with that belief. What opportunities and experiences will open up for you? Does it feel better than the first vision?

It may seem simple but when you keep running the two exercises over and over again, your brain will link more pleasure to the positive belief and throw out the negative ones.

BENEFITS

When you buy something, you do not just buy the product or service for what it does. You also choose it because of other intangible things that it will give you. For example, when you buy a new car you are interested in its features like engine size and fuel efficiency, but you also think about the benefits the car will bring to your image and lifestyle.

When companies market products and services, they focus on the benefits that buyers will get from using them. You can use the same highly effective tactics when you are selling yourself to potential employers. For example if you are aged over 40 - a feature - you can bring the benefits of experience and maturity to any role.

So, what is the difference? A feature is something about you — it is a fact, like your age. In isolation, a fact has little or no significance. You state a fact when you say, 'I m 45 years old'. A benefit on the other hand is something that can be delivered because a feature exists. For example, 'I m 45 years old which means that I have over 20 years of experience in this industry'. Someone reading this on your CV would immediately see why and how your age is important in delivering the benefit of experience.

It is important to sell yourself by your benefits because we are used to responding to sales messages all the time and because people always want to know what is in it for them. By keeping focus on your benefits, a potential employer can see quickly why they should choose you.

So now, make a list of five facts about yourself and write at least one benefit for each one. When you write to potential employers or attend interviews, you are ready and prepared to discuss the benefits of hiring you.

BLUES

The benefit of a national holiday like Christmas is that everyone has something pleasant to focus on and this creates a sense of collective goodwill. The pleasure that we experience in the run up to Christmas is about anticipation and excitement — exactly the same as when we have anything to look forward to. Once the Christmas holiday is over, we get back to the routine of life. This is like returning from your summer holidays except that it seems worse at this time of year because of the cold weather, dark nights and an empty bank account. **The blues begin!**

101 Ways to Love Your Job

It is common to feel fed up in the New Year because it is a traditional time to review your progress in life and doubtless focus on what you have not yet achieved. These negative feelings are fuelled by New Year resolutions to give up all the 'bad' habits that you have.

The solution is to create something nice to focus on. Make a note of all the good reasons you originally took your job and the benefits you get from it. Next, think about ways in which you can make your life more fulfilling. Perhaps there are outstanding tasks you have been putting off? Getting on top of these will make you feel good about yourself — and that is your aim.

Keep yourself busy outside of work too. Continue the social life you enjoyed over the holidays by visiting friends and family. Make sure you regularly do things you enjoy so that, even if you cannot love your job, you have other pleasurable things to do each week.

Commit to activities outside of work and enjoy the anticipation of looking forward to them. Then, when you do them, you can enjoy them all over again.

BOSSES

We cannot always choose our bosses. Even if they recruited us, they may be promoted or leave. Even if they stay our boss, sometimes working together can be completely different from what we expect from the interview. Getting on with your boss can be a cause of stress, especially if they control your workload and can change your priorities at a moment s notice. They can also have a big influence on your career within the organisation. So how can you make your life simpler and easier by managing your boss?

We tend to like and trust people who are similar to us. Therefore, by adopting a similar working style to your boss you can build trust and

19

mutual respect quickly. Take a look at yourself and your boss from an observer s position. Are your working styles similar or very different? Is their desk tidy? Do they keep their diary up-to-date with every move? How does this compare with yours?

Do they like you to report to them in detail or do they only want broad overviews? Do they have a very formal way of working or do they prefer a more relaxed atmosphere? How do their preferences compare to your style of working?

If you identify that your styles of working are very different, this could be an area where you can adjust what you do in order to be more like your boss. This is not to encourage you to become a 'clone' of your boss but, if your working styles are more similar then you will be trusted to work in the way that you want to.

BOUNDARIES

Desert explorers can be thousands of miles away from another human being or animal. Even so, they will erect a tent at night. The canvas or nylon may be too thin to keep out the weather. The simple act of retreating inside something that has a defined boundary gives them a feeling of security.

You have boundaries at work. They may be formally defined within your job description or, they may just exist as a result of custom and practice. You can consider them as aiding your security, allowing you and others to know how far you are expected to go. You can also consider them as being restrictions to your freedom of action and initiative.

These two viewpoints can happily exist together. Once you are in the habit of doing your job with excellence and within your boundaries, and only then, you can explore subtle ways of gradually expanding them to give you more creative job satisfaction.

Notice that sequence. First operate within and only then seek to expand.

You need an acute awareness of the attitudes of your work colleagues and bosses. There is no future in annoying them by your actions. Be aware of the narrow borderline or boundary between 'taking the law into your own hands' and 'showing initiative'.

You may not always have a view of the fuller picture, so approach boundary expansion by simply asking before doing. Do not allow your question to push others into a corner, instead, keep them open by asking, 'Can I have your opinion on an idea. How would it be if?'.

BULLYING

Bullying comes in many forms. If it happens in schools (and we all know that it does) then it will happen in organisations and companies, simply because bullies grow up. Bullies do not pick on everyone; they choose targets that they think they can intimidate because bullying is all about power.

So how do you avoid becoming a victim? You need to build up your own self-esteem so that your body language gives out the message that you are confident and not a likely target for bullying. You might want to get help with this from a coach. Practise being assertive and saying 'no' when you are in a safe environment so that you will not feel awkward when faced with a challenge.

You must make sure that you are clear about your own beliefs concerning the correct behaviour for you. Then if someone is behaving in a way that you think is inappropriate to you, you can be confident enough to challenge that individual. It does not matter if they think they are behaving appropriately, if their conduct upsets you, then you do not have to put up with it.

You must tell others what is happening to you. Most victims think that they have somehow caused the problem or that others will accuse them of imagining things. They often do not tell anyone, putting up with it for months before finally cracking. You need not, and must not, let that happen to you.

Either talk to your boss, or get support from colleagues. If your boss is bullying you, then seek advice from someone independent, like the Citizens Advice Bureau, to find out what action you could take.

Everyone has the right to be happy at work and not be subjected to harassment in any form.

CARE

Apparently, stress causes more absenteeism from work than any other illness. There is certainly the potential for stress at work, so what action can you take to care for yourself by controlling your levels of stress?

Firstly, look at what causes your stress. Do certain people or situations make you feel more stressed than others? This is really an issue of what you are focusing on — just like people who see a glass half empty or half full — they are focusing on what has gone or what is left. In the same way, you can focus on what is bad or what is good. Control your focus by reframing anything negative into a positive until it becomes a habit for you to think about the positive first.

Are you stressed because you have too much to do? Do you have too much to do because you did not say no to someone, or is it because you put off doing tasks until the deadlines were looming? If so, you need to develop assertiveness and time management skills.

Next, how do you deal with stress? Are you in the habit of staying late at work and not taking a break for lunch? This will actually make you less effective in the long term because both your body and mind need rest periods.

When you finally leave work for the day, what do you do to relax? What exercise do you take, or do you just have enough energy to get home? Do you eat fresh fruit and vegetables every day or do you rely on ready meals because you are too tired to cook? What hobbies could you start so that you do not spend all your evenings and weekends thinking about work? You may think you do not have the time, but if you make the effort to improve your life outside of work, you will be amazed at how much better you will feel.

COACHING

Coaching is a hot topic in the media. Life Coaching is about borrowing something that has been used on the sports field for decades. It is using the skills of a coach to help you make all areas of your life what you want them to be.

I think the current interest in coaching stems from finding ourselves in a competitive environment. Often without our families around us, we no longer have the support networks that we and earlier generations once took for granted. Previously, people would take a job for life and a senior colleague would help steer them through their career. Now we change jobs and careers more frequently and this mentoring is often lacking.

So what does a coach do? A coach reminds you to congratulate yourself when you do something well and also helps you identify where you could improve. Coaches work in every aspect of life including work, home, relationships and sport. Coaches help you to achieve the goals you set yourself, no matter what their context.

There are a couple of things that coaching is not. Coaching is NOT about telling someone what to do or judging them. It is sometimes useful for a coach to have had experience of what you are going through, but at other times it is better if not, as this allows your coach to focus totally on you and your situation without drawing parallels from their own life.

So, what is the difference between a coach and a best friend? Your coach will not remind you of past failures or tell you why you should not aim for a goal. Your coach will use their training to help you identify your goals clearly, to decide what you need to do to reach each goal and then work with you to keep you on track until you achieve it.

Even the best of friends may have a hidden agenda or a tendency to gossip. Your professional life coach has neither and every coaching session is in absolute confidentiality. By definition, a friend is part of your past. **Your coach is interested in the now and your future.**

CHALLENGE

Confident people are positive people. They have positive thoughts about themselves and others. They notice the positive aspects of situations rather than the negative ones. When you feel that you lack confidence, your self-talk will tend to mirror this.

This is a vicious circle of our feelings reflecting our thoughts and dictating our behaviour. When we think negative things, we feel unhappy and behave in an unconfident way.

Just like going on a detox regime to lose weight and clear your body of toxins, you can break this vicious circle by going on a seven-day negativity fast. Accept this challenge.

So what do you do? For seven consecutive days, you can ONLY say positive things about yourself or others. If you catch yourself being negative then you have to start from the beginning again.

Boost your commitment by telling people that you are doing it. Then they can help you by pointing out any time that you say anything negative. You must be honest and never cheat by being negative when you are alone!

You may find that you do not say much to start with! This is only because you have got into the habit of focusing on the negative aspects of situations. It does not take long to break a habit and soon your subconscious mind will start presenting you with positive things to say. As a result, you will feel much more positive and confident.

Here are a few **high negative words** to avoid:- could, should, would, might, try, cannot, would not, should not, no way.

Each time that you find yourself saying - **or even thinking** - any of these, pause, correct yourself and select words from; can, will, now, yes!

CHANGES
Most of us will change jobs several times during our working lives. Sometimes this will involve moves within the same industry or within the same type of work. However, it is also highly likely that some of those job changes will involve a completely new career.

A career change may be forced upon you due to the decline of your industry. Alternatively, you may decide to pursue something that is more rewarding. Perhaps redundancy has given you the time and money to take stock and decide what you want to do with the rest of your working life.

So where do you start? Make a list of everything you like and dislike about your current job. As well as specific aspects, like long lunch breaks or a difficult boss. Include generalities like 'working on my own' or 'responsibility for budgets'. Next, make a list of your strengths and weaknesses and be strictly honest with yourself. It is pointless to spend years in a job that forces you to use skills that do not come easily and effortlessly to you.

Now take time to dream. If there were no financial limitations or other restrictions, what work would you do? What are your hobbies — why do you love spending time on them? How much income do you truly need, compared with what you would like? Determine your priorities in as many areas as possible.

Now, thinking about your strengths and the things that you love doing, how could you use these skills in a job that you could be really passionate about? The next step is to research the possibilities that you have identified to find out what you have to do in order to make the career move that is right for you.

CLARITY

When you say something, you know what you mean. Hopefully, you also mean what you say. But do others always know what you mean?

If someone uses a PC to send a message to someone with an Apple Mac computer, what leaves the PC may be vastly different from what arrives at the Apple Mac, simply because each computer uses a different system to process its information.

People too, use different systems. An academic will use different words from a tradesman. A politician will use different words from a journalist. They can speak to each other, but each may take a totally different meaning from what is said.

This can happen at work too. If you are not totally clear about what you are asked to do, repeat back your understanding of the task in your own words, for confirmation that you have total understanding of the situation.

When you ask someone to do something else for you, invite them to summarise what they are to do in their own words. This procedure will take a few moments but it will add clarity so that you will deliver or receive exactly what is expected.

Suppose that you are asked to do something on Monday. Your boss says, 'I need it on my desk next Wednesday'. Some people mean in two days time. Others will think of two days ahead as 'this Wednesday' so they mean that your deadline is actually nine days away. If you both agree that your deadline is Wednesday 24th you will have clarity.

When the boss says 'Wednesday' he may mean by 8am when he gets to work. You may think he means 5pm before you go home. Achieve clarity by confirming, 'Wednesday 24th at 8am'.

Clarity and the use of simple words can help you to avoid pitfalls at work.

COMMUNICATIONS
Most difficulties arise between people because of a misunderstanding of communication. Poor communication can create confusion, cause mistakes and even foster mistrust between yourself and your boss or your colleagues.

Fortunately, there has been research into different styles of communication and if you are willing to behave flexibly to make sure you understand and are understood, you can easily improve your communication skills.

One of the most common causes of misunderstanding is when people talk in very general terms about a task, but then do not give detail about how they expect it to be carried out or how much progress reporting they expect on the way. Unfortunately, people interpret general statements in different ways and may not carry out tasks in the way that the boss had hoped. This can lead to frustration on both sides and a reluctance to trust each other in future projects.

Some people suffer from poor communication by not really knowing what their boss wants from them, and by constantly feeling that they are not doing their job satisfactorily. The way to solve misunderstanding is to ask many questions — particularly when you are given a new task. One of the most powerful questions to ask is the open question, for example, 'what specifically would you like me to do?'

Sometimes you will get an unhelpful answer like 'If I tell you, I might as well do it myself'! This is a quite common retort from someone who does not like to deal in detail. (Or who does not know what they really want until you come up with what they do not want!) Unfortunately, this is when you need to be brave and explain that, in order to do an excellent job, you really do need more guidance regarding their expectations, rather than instructions about how to do a task. You are asking them to define the expected results, rather than how to get to there.

If you tackle any vague task that you are given in this courageous way, you will minimise misunderstanding and reduce stress for all concerned.

CONFIDENCE
When you have a knock to your confidence - like being made redundant or failing to get a job - it can cause you to doubt yourself

and your abilities. If you are not feeling 100% confident, how can you quickly boost your self-esteem and rebuild your confidence?

Have you ever noticed when you have bought a new car, that suddenly you start seeing the same make and model on the road? That is because whilst you were going through the buying process your mind was filtering every reference to that car whenever possible and bringing it to your awareness.

In the same way, if you have taken a knock to your confidence, your mind is likely to be running all sorts of questioning like 'Why has this happened to me?' 'What am I going to do?' and so on. You will probably notice that your inner voice is sounding weak and frightened and like a whining child!

Because your mind is thinking negative thoughts, it will be filtering everything positive that happens to you and focusing on the negative things. This is a vicious circle that needs to be interrupted so that you can feel empowered to pick yourself up and start solving your problem. So how do you do it?

Firstly, just as you would if you did not like a TV show, turn down the volume of your negative inner voice or change the channel! When you start thinking negative thoughts, you will probably find that your body language becomes just like a depressed person s— slumped and focusing down to the ground. So, employ some 'reverse feedback'. Stand up like a confident person, put your shoulders back, hold your head up high and walk around briskly. Act positive to feel positive.

When you are in this state you can ask yourself the questions that will help you solve your current situation. Replace 'why', with 'what, how and when'. 'What do I need to do to feel good?' or, 'What can I do to solve this?'

CONFLICT

Do you ever suffer from wanting to do things, but never following through on them?

We would usually put this down to procrastination or another excuse such as lack of time, money or energy. However, the reason you do not achieve some of the things that you want to do, can be due to an internal conflict between your conscious and subconscious minds.

An internal conflict is caused by your subconscious mind trying to protect you and attaching pain to doing this thing that your conscious mind wants to do. An example would be if you want to go to the gym and you know you will feel relaxed when you have been — but you just cannot find the way to get off the sofa. Sound familiar? You need to find out why your subconscious is stopping you.

Ask yourself what your subconscious mind s positive intention could be for NOT doing the thing you want to do. You will probably be thinking, 'I do not know'. But imagine, if you did know, what do you think would be the answer? You may be surprised by the answer and usually it does not make sense on a conscious level. For example, if you want to go to the gym to feel relaxed, your subconscious may be stopping you because it thinks that sitting on the sofa is relaxing!

Therefore, as with any conflict, you need to negotiate a compromise that both sides are happy with. Write down as many ways as you can think that you could solve the conflict — how could you ensure that you are relaxed when you finish at the gym and have the chilling out time you need on the sofa?

If you can solve your internal conflicts, there will be nothing to stop you doing everything that you want to do.

CONTENTMENT

What can you do to make yourself feel more content?

The truth is that you get what you focus on. Therefore, if you focus on feeling depressed and sad, you will notice everything that happens around you that supports this sadness. The first thing to do is to make a list of what is good in your life. Remember that every negative has a positive opposite meaning — for example if you are in debt, that means that people trust you to pay them back.

Have you ever noticed that if you are at work and feeling unhappy and a customer calls, you can suddenly change and become friendly and happy? That is known as leverage. If you really cannot imagine ever feeling happy again, then pretend that you have to spend all day with a customer or someone who you have to be jolly with.

Try some of these techniques to make yourself happier. For the next seven days commit to say only positive things — about yourself and about others.

Read or listen to the news at the end of the day - if at all - rather than at the beginning. The news is often negative and you do not want to start your day feeling sad.

Treat yourself to something you love doing at least once a week. Before long, you will notice yourself feeling a lot happier.

CREATIVITY

Unlocking your creative side can help in many ways — it can help you write a more interesting report, it can help you find alternative solutions to problems and it can help you define the best job for you.

So why does it need unlocking? We each have two sides to our brains — the left and the right. The left side is our logical, analytical side that is stimulated during education. The right side is our intuitive, imaginative side which is all too often blocked. Although some jobs require us to use the left side of the brain, we are far more effective in everything we do if we use both sides of our brain.

There are many ways to unlock your right brain. These include listening to music, drawing, playing games, visualising and imagining.

You could even copy one of the world s most celebrated creative minds. Walt Disney had separate rooms where he would work on new ideas. In one room he allowed the right side of his brain to let his imagination run free without criticism. Then he would move to another room to use his left brain to plan how to achieve his dreams.

How could you use this to increase your creativity? You could anchor creative feelings, for example using clothes, rooms, simple rituals or carefully chosen people. So, if you need to wear certain clothes in order to feel creative, then do that. Or if you need to be with certain people to be creative, then get together with them.

Creativity is a state of mind. We can all do it. Our brains are just like other muscles in our body, they need exercising to keep them fit and active. The key to creativity is to start to do something. You may not know where your creativity may take you, but this does not mean that you are lost. You are just exploring!

CUSTOMERS

One of the most important things you need to do when you want a career change or to become self-employed, is to find new customers or employers who want to use your services.

Whether you want a job or new customers, the process is the same. The first thing you need to do is to build up a database of your experience. Where have you worked before? What industries have you worked in? What were the sizes of the companies — small or large? What departments did you work in, what job titles did you have, what were your main tasks, what projects were you involved in?

Collect all of this information together and also add in things that interest you — these may be hobbies that you have never received payment for, but you may have a lot of knowledge about these areas. Once you have done this, get clear in your mind what it is you are offering to your potential customers or employers.

Next, you can research the names and addresses of potential customers or employers. I look in local directories — the Chamber of Commerce or Reference Library are good sources of these directories — and do not forget the Yellow Pages and Thompson Local Directory. Look at recruitment pages to see which local companies are advertising. Then you can phone them to find out the name of the person who would be your best contact.

Once you have this information, you begin contacting them to make them aware of your services. This process may take some time as they may not have an immediate need, but, once they know about you, there is always the chance that something will happen. If they do not know you are there, they cannot possibly call you!

CV

Once you have started down the self-improvement route, you might find that you want to move on to another job and this means that you need to update your CV with everything that you have achieved since you last wrote it.

Do you need to add any qualifications you have recently acquired? This is time to abbreviate your earliest qualifications? If you have many years of experience, you only need to give details of your most recent results, for example, BA (Hons) Photography - Oxford University. Your earlier details are not as important as they once were, so just say '5 O-Levels' without giving grades or subjects.

Unless you have just left school, you can also leave out the details of schools and colleges you attended but, do include vocational or trade qualifications and courses that are relevant to the job that you seek.

Next, list your work history starting with the most recent. Do not leave any large gaps of time unexplained. (The reader may think you were unemployed - or worse). If you were unemployed for a period, mention any courses or voluntary work that you did to help you find work. If you had a period of bringing up a family, mention any part-time work you did.

For each job that you have had, list your main responsibilities and highlight any personal job related achievements. Include examples of teamwork as well as solo initiatives.

The aim of your CV is to get you an interview and therefore it needs to promote you in a positive manner. Do not make up achievements or lie, but do include things that will make a potential interviewer want to meet you.

Always include a brief mention of your hobbies and interests. It gives the interviewer more information about you and gives them something to ask you about at the start of the interview to relax you.

DECISIONS

Changing jobs is one of life's major decisions. Think of the type of work you would enjoy the most. After all, you spend most of your waking life at work, so it is best to enjoy it!

You may wonder why it matters whether you enjoy your work. If you are interested in the products or services that your employer sells then it makes you a more useful, valuable and knowledgeable employee. You are more likely to make extra effort to help others when you enjoy your work and, you will be happier outside work as well.

Think about what interests you. What hobbies do you have, what books do you like to read, how do you like to spend your free time? Do you want a job where you are doing many different things, or do you prefer to concentrate on one task at a time? Do you like to work with people or do you prefer to work on your own? Are you happier using your hands or your head - or both?

What is important to you at work? Do you value taking responsibility or do you prefer not to? Write down 10 things about the work you would like to do and that are important for you to feel fulfilled and happy there.

If you are really stuck for ideas about this, then think about what you would hate instead. Write down all the things that would make you want to leave a job. Usually the opposite of the things you hate are the things that would make you most happy.

Spending this extra time thinking about what you could do and enjoy will pay dividends. The more you know yourself, the more likely you are to make better decisions about the kind of work that you accept.

ENTHUSIASM

You will surely have seen a typical stroppy teenager. Perhaps you were one!

They are asked to do something and are not yet confident enough with their impending adulthood to refuse. So they do it with an air of boredom, sulkiness and droop shouldered, quivering lip, insolence.

Of course, you soon grew out of this behaviour. But not everyone has. When you replace 'acceptance' with 'enthusiasm' you will create amazing results. An enthusiastic person is liked, respected and often promoted over their equally competent but more lethargic colleagues.

Displaying enthusiasm is one of those rare situations where it is permissible to fake it until you make it. Stand tall and alert as you would if you felt truly enthusiastic. Smile and nod as you would with genuine enthusiasm. Move with a positive sense of purpose. In a very short period, your physiognomy or body language will induce a subtle but genuine shift of attitude and you will be enthusiastic.

Do not be embarrassed to spend time alone in front of a mirror. Assume a hangdog expression and stance, the way you did as that unpleasant adolescent, think [briefly] of some sad occasion. Note how you look. Now stand tall, think happy thoughts, be pert and alert. Note the difference. Which of the two would you rather work with?

Each day at work, you have a choice. You can be a miserable victim of circumstance or you can approach every task with an air of enthusiasm. The job will not change. Your attitude to it will and so will the attitude of those who have to work with you. If you have to be there from nine-to-five, decide to enjoy your time as much as you can. Enthusiasm is the key.

ESCAPE

Everyone experiences the odd 'bad hair day' and that occasional 'Monday morning feeling'. If, on your way to work, you just know that this is going to be 'another of those days', what will you do about it?

Very often in life, we seem to attract to us what we expect. Expect to have a bad day, and that is exactly what you will get. Far better then, to raise your hopes and expect a good day. But what if the bad days outnumber the good ones? Then you need to ask yourself this simple question, 'Why stick at a job that you do not enjoy?'.

You may imagine that your choices are limited by the need to earn a certain salary or wage to meet your debts and obligations. You may experience sheer stubbornness that you will stick to a decision you made before, even if this means that you simply exist Monday to Friday so that you can truly 'live' at the weekends. Stay in a situation like this and you are still making a choice. The choice to do nothing.

You can escape! Perhaps you think that you could not cope without your current job. If you were suddenly fired or made redundant it would not be a pleasant experience for a while but, like millions of others, you would cope and you would find another job. If you accept the truth of this, then you also accept the truth that change is possible.

Part of your escape plan is to decide what you would do for a living if there were no restraints or limitations at all. You might not reach that ideal situation in a single leap, but you can certainly choose an occupation that will move you ever closer to it.

Make your decision to escape to a better life. Define the actions that you can take to get you there. It is good to do a job that you love. It is even better to love the job that you do. Here is a useful tip to get you thinking along escapology lines. What would you do for the love of it, without pay? How could you turn that idea into a job that someone will pay you to do?

EVALUATION

Some people feel guilty when everything is going well, almost as if they should not find things so easy. This is an indication that evaluation is needed.

Evaluate your belief about what you deserve. If you have any doubts about deserving the good things that are in your life, these doubts will affect your happiness, inner peace and contentment.

When you feel that you do not deserve what you have, you will be constantly worrying it will be taken from you at any moment. It is really important to sort this attitude out because it will affect how you negotiate at work for things like your salary and job description.

Think about someone you love — maybe your partner, your child or parent or sibling. Do you think they deserve exactly what they have or more? Would you want them to suffer? Why not? Is it because you love them? Would someone who loved you want you to suffer? Therefore, why do you think you should suffer? Perhaps you learnt as a child that 'bad people have things easy and good people have to suffer'. If you identify with this erroneous belief, ditch it right now!

If you do not value yourself, then how can others value you? Start by accepting compliments. When someone compliments you on something, say thank you. Do not say, 'what this old thing?' or, 'oh it was easy, anyone could have done it'. These put-down replies suggest that the person complimenting you was wrong to do so and you would not want to make someone else feel bad, would you?

EXPECTATIONS

Your beliefs affect your thoughts, your emotions and your behaviour. In the same way, what you expect to happen usually ends up becoming true.

Several experiments have proved this belief. A new schoolteacher entering her class of 8 year olds for the first time was told that a small group of the children in the class were gifted . The children were unaware of the label they had been given. By the end of the term these gifted pupils were found to have performed significantly better than the rest of the class. The teacher said how responsive she had found this group and how rewarding it had been to teach them. These children had performed better because their teacher had expected them to and they had risen to meet her expectations with improved performance.

This shows two things; our expectations of people shape the way we treat them, and that treatment shapes the way people respond to us.

Thinking back to your school days, did you work harder for different teachers? Were there subjects that became more interesting from one year to the next? Was this due to a change in teacher?

In the same way, at work our performance can change dramatically under different managers. However, you do not have to be a victim to your manager s low expectations of him/herself or you — you can choose to create your own expectations.

What are your expectations about your career? Are they positive? Do you need to change them? What are the expectations of those people you spend most time with? The saying if you lie down with dogs, you ll get up with fleas is true. Surround yourself with people who have positive expectations for themselves. Expect the best from, and for, yourself and those around you and see the change in yours and others performance.

FAKING

There was a successful television series called 'Faking It'. It was about people doing things that they did not believe they would ever be able to do. In the same way that the people in the show behaved differently, compared with their normal conduct, you do not have to BE confident and assertive; you can DO confidence and assertiveness instead. Your subconscious mind cannot recognise the difference between acting and reality. Actions cause feelings, so when you act as if you are confident, you will end up feeling confident.

So how do you 'do' confidence and assertiveness? One way is to copy or model someone who appears confident. Do you know someone like that? Watch them and notice everything that they do and say, observe their body language. What do they do differently from you? How could you change your behaviour to behave more like them in situations where you want to appear more confident?

Confident people believe certain things about themselves and their rights. These are beliefs that you can define, develop and take on board. For example, confident people believe that they are entitled to their own opinions and feelings and that it is OK to disagree with others. They even believe that it is OK not to have an opinion about everything!

FEAR

Fear. We all suffer from it from time to time. Maybe a specific event in the past or future fills us with fear when we think about it. Fear affects us in different ways — it may stop some of us from doing something or, to simply endure experiences that we might otherwise enjoy.

Firstly, you need to identify why you are afraid. Are you scared of failing? Or are you afraid of succeeding? Are you scared of not being perfect? At the base of most fears is the fear of not being able to cope with whatever happens to you.

I have read that the word fear can be an acronym of False Expectation Appearing Real. I like this description because we all have the ability to exaggerate the possible ways that things can go wrong and then represent them as facts.

So, thinking about the event that causes you to feel fearful, imagine what is the worst that can happen? Is that so bad? Research has found that over 90% of what we worry about never happens and most of what we worry about today, we also worried about yesterday — so isn t it time we gave ourselves a break?

Fear is a sign that you are learning and growing. Remember when you were learning to drive? The first time the instructor told you to change gears? Did it feel comfortable at first? Did it take a little time before you could change gears without looking? Were not the rewards worth that effort? It is the same with other areas of your life. Fear lets us know that we are doing something new and that we have some learning and preparation to do.

The only way to beat your fears is to do whatever you are fearful of and trust that whatever happens to you, you will be able to handle it.

FEEDBACK

So you attended the interview or meeting, you did your best and you did not get the job or desired result.

If it is possible, phone the others involved and ask them to tell you why you were unsuccessful. Ask them to help you be successful in the future by giving you valuable feedback - this will ensure that their feedback is positive. You may have dealings with them in the future and this extra interest will stand you in good stead.

Whether or not you can get the feedback, think over the event as if you were a fly on the wall — did you present yourself in the best possible way? What signals did the other people give? With hindsight, were you the best person for the job? Do not compare yourself to the other candidates. You could have been rejected for any number of possible reasons, including that the successful candidate was cheaper!

Above all, remember that you have loads to offer any future employer or client — maybe all you need is to work on how you communicate your proposition so that they can understand you better?

Use all feedback to turn stumbling blocks into stepping stones.

FITNESS

Your personal goals probably include something about getting your body fit. But what about making sure you keep your mind fit too?

If there is a possibility of redundancy, the staff of most value to the organisation will be in the strongest position. So, it is wise to ensure that you maintain your mental fitness whether your job may be at risk, or if you simply want to develop your career further.

You need a plan of action to keep your mental fitness developed. Because the world seems to move faster today, if you are not developing yourself, you are probably falling behind everyone else, rather than standing still.

Start by reading books and journals about your particular industry or profession. Investigate courses that you can attend through your organisation including vocational training, new technology and personal development. Check evening classes at local colleges. Consider taking further qualifications. It is possible to study for a degree part time by collecting 'units' of study and you do not necessarily need academic qualifications to be eligible.

Improving your mental fitness keeps your brain active, helps you live a more fulfilling, longer life and improves your career prospects. And, it must surely be better than watching television every evening.

FREEDOM

Feeling trapped in your job? Craving freedom?

Sometimes we feel that there are no other options for us but to stay in the same job — whether we believe that we could not earn as much money, or that no one would employ us at our age. We may daydream of winning the lottery and leaving work for good. But you can stay as you are and feel free now.

Firstly, you must acknowledge that you create your own reality. If you believe that the weather in March is always cold and wet, your brain will filter out any dry sunny days so that your belief remains intact. It is the same with how you feel about your job — what you focus on becomes your reality. So if you believe that your company exploits you, your brain will filter out all the nice things they do and highlight only the things that confirm your belief about being exploited.

If you do not believe me, try an experiment. Look around your room and really notice everything that is blue. Now close your eyes and remind yourself of everything that is brown. Unless you know the room you are in very well, you will have difficulty with this because your brain was searching for blue! This shows how you focus most on what you think about most, to the exclusion of other thoughts. Focus on positive things about any situation where you feel trapped.

Another thing you can do is to carry out a reality check. List all the other options you could follow if you chose to. Some people put money away in a separate bank account they call their 'Freedom

Fund'. This helps them to feel free to choose to work rather than having to work because they have no other options.

Finally, make time to spend doing things you love to do as well as the things you have to do — everyone needs fun time.

GOALS

Research has found that those who set written goals are richer and more successful than those who do not. We should set goals for ourselves that are inspiring, believable, visible, time targeted and stretching.

Firstly, you have to identify your goals. Take a notebook and write down everything that you want to be, do and have. Then choose four or five goals that you can work on now.

After you have chosen your goals, ask yourself the following questions with regard to each one:-

How will reaching this goal affect me and those around me?

Is it morally right and fair to everyone concerned?

Will I make sure it happens?

Am I merely hoping this will happen?

Am I going to do this or am I just trying?

What do I have to do to achieve this goal?

What action am I going to take now to start the process of making it happen?

Read your goal list twice daily, aloud, each morning and evening. Do something towards their achievement every day. Some goals will be large and it can help to split them into smaller chunks. Create a mental image of you having already achieved your goal. This will keep your goal firmly in your mind. Finally, act as if it is impossible to fail in reaching your goal — your brain will obey you!

HABITS

Bullying, like any behaviour, is a habit. And any habit can be broken.

Often a habit is something we just find ourselves doing. For example, smokers often find themselves reaching for a cigarette when they sit down with a drink. The first step to breaking a habit is to become aware of how often you do it.

Human beings are only motivated by two things — to avoid pain or to gain pleasure. It is likely that, as a bully, you stop yourself from feeling bad by making someone else feel bad instead. This is just a pattern of behaviour and does not mean that you are a bad person who cannot change.

Start your own confidential behaviour journal. Note down all the times that you are aggressive to other people and the circumstances surrounding the behaviour and the feelings you have at the time. Who or what triggers your aggression? You will soon start to see a pattern emerging. Perhaps, when you feel pressured by your boss, you pass this onto other people. Note down the people that you behave aggressively towards. Do you find it easier to pick on some rather than others? Why? Write down what you actually say and do at these times.

The next step is to decide what result you try to achieve by your behaviour. How you could get the same result by behaving in a different way?

Aggression and bullying usually hide a lack of confidence. If you feel unsure of your own ability and find that this is the trigger that starts your negative behaviour, read books on self-discovery or book a session with a coach about improving your self-esteem. Seek help to break your habit and you will be much happier. So will your staff, your family and work colleagues.

HAPPINESS

Once you have identified what you need to do to improve the balance in your life, your ongoing challenge is to maintain the balance on a daily basis so that you can achieve all your dreams and goals with lasting happiness.

Every time you want to do something new or add something else to your life, you can check against your wheel (See the section on Balance) to see whether it would benefit the areas you have identified.

If it would benefit most areas, then you can be sure that the balance will be affected in a positive way. If it would detract from more areas than it would benefit, you know that your balance will be affected in a negative way. For example, you may be asked to take on a new role at work that involves lots of travelling and staying away from home. This may benefit the career and financial sections of your wheel, but will it benefit your relationships, family, exercise and hobby sections?

It is simplistic to say that if something does not benefit most of your sections that you should not do it. You may really want to do or have that thing or you may feel under pressure to reach for it. The beauty of using the wheel is that, like a compass, you can keep checking that you are on course. Then you can fall back on your skills as a negotiator so that you can satisfy each area and still achieve what you want.

By using this disciplined approach you can achieve everything you want in your life without sacrificing any areas that are important to you. How badly do you want a good career if you do not have a relationship left at the end of it?

HOLIDAYS

Every August and January, the shops promote 'Back to School' items like uniforms and stationery, which means that the holidays will soon be over. It made me think that, because holidays are a time for rest and relaxation, they give you time away from your immediate current situation to take a birds' eye overview as you consider your circumstances. So, whether you are definitely thinking of a career change or just want to check that your career is on track, follow these simple guidelines.

Start by making a list of everything that is important to you at work, for example creativity. This will give you a list of values in your work. Next, score each value out of ten, according to how satisfied you are with its delivery in your current role. Use 10 for 'extremely satisfied' and 1 for 'not satisfied at all'.

Next, write down what a level 10 satisfaction would feel like for each of these values. This is the same type of visualisation that athletes do when then are mentally preparing for competition — they imagine the perfect race, throw, jump or other outcome. Imagining what you want prepares the mind and body to recognise it when it comes along.

The last part of this exercise is to write down three tasks for each area that define what you could do to take you closer to scoring 10 for each value and set yourself a date by which you will have achieved them. For example, you may want to book a meeting with your boss.

Doing this exercise will help you identify areas that need your focus to create more satisfaction in your work.

HOMEWORK

If you are attracted by the idea of working from home and becoming your own boss, you will need to consider the financial implications.

Do you have savings or equity in your home that you can fall back on? If not, you need to explore the options of getting finance from banks or grants or possibly family and friends. Small business advisers and books on self-employment can point you in the right direction to explore these further. Do not go straight to your bank without shopping around first to see if there are better deals available.

Can you cut down your expenses so that you reduce your outgoings for the first few months? Could you consider fixing your mortgage rate so that you know what your outgoings will be for a while? Do you have your family s support for launching your new venture? If they support you, it will be much easier for them to accept the reduced financial situation.

Where will you work? Will you work from home or do you need to find premises? If you are planning to work from home, is there an area of the house that you can devote to the business? Can you shut the door on this area so that you can forget about work in the evenings and weekends? How many hours are you willing to work? Be prepared to work longer hours initially and consider whether your relationships and social life will tolerate this.

It is always best to look at the potential obstacles when you are starting out so that you can answer any questions that arise

IDEALS

There are many jobs advertised and if you are in search of work, it can be tempting to take the first one that you are offered. However, not all jobs are equal. Finding your ideal job is a bit like finding your ideal partner — some thought beforehand of what you want helps you make better decisions.

Firstly, ask yourself what is important to you at work. Write down at least 10 things, for example, 'being part of a team' or 'using my own initiative'. When you have your list, take the first two things that you wrote down and decide which one is the more important. Do this all the way down the list and you will end up with a hierarchy of values that are important to you at work.

You can use this list to find out if your ideals match the job. For example, if you value being part of a team but most of the work is done alone, this may not suit you.

Now list what you love. What are you passionate about and interested in? An ideal job combines your skills with your passion. Some employment specialists claim that it is easier to recruit attitude and train in aptitude than the other way around. If you are passionate about what you are doing, your attitude will be the right one for the company.

Armed with this increased knowledge of yourself, start targeting those companies that appeal to you by offering a near match to your values and interests. You do not have to wait until they are recruiting - write to them now, mentioning why you are applying to them.

If you are not successful, ask them for advice on how you could be successful in the future. If you are really interested in working for them, do not give up until you get what you want!

IMPRESS

First impressions are very important and you want to maximise your chance of being offered the job once you get to the interview — after all, you have done the hard part of getting through the application form sifting!

When deciding what to wear to an interview, it is always best to be understated. Even if the office or store you want to work in is very trendy, it is still more advisable to wear a suit — you can always add a trendy tie or brooch to your outfit to show your appreciation of their dress code.

It is also a good idea to stick to neutral colours like blue, grey or black. I don t often make generalisations, but some people hate bright colours and this will affect their judgement of you from the beginning. In addition, a good suit in a neutral colour is a staple item of your wardrobe that can be worn many times.

Once you have decided on the suit, remember to think about the details of your outfit. Firstly, make sure your shoes are polished and re-heeled if necessary. Ladies, opt for a mid-height heel. Does your handbag look big enough to hold the kitchen sink? Buy a smaller one for the interview, but make sure that it can fit in a spare pair of tights in case you ladder them on the way to the interview. Make sure your nails are clean and not too long and that they are manicured. If you bite your nails, tidy them up and rub some cream into them to soften the hard skin around them. If you are going to wear nail polish, opt for a neutral colour. Lastly, get your hair cut or trimmed and wash it on the morning of the interview. If you suffer from dandruff when nervous, get a medicated shampoo and carry a clothes brush with you to the interview!

When you look the part, you will feel confident to represent yourself in the best way in the interview.

INDEPENDENCE

One way to change careers is to change from being an employee to becoming independent and self-employed. Indeed, some forecasters predict that more of us will choose this option as the 'job for life' culture disappears.

So, you are tempted by the thought of being your own boss? The first thing to do is to identify why you want to be self-employed. There are many different reasons for this and you need to make sure that whatever your reasons, they will be strong enough to carry you through the tough times.

Next, what is your business idea? Even if you will be leaving employment to contract your services back to the same organisation, you should still consider other companies and their needs for your services — is the market large enough for you to gain more clients as you go along? How many competitors do you have in this area?

If you will be leaving to start up in complete independence, decide how you will market your new business to gain new clients. Think about enlarging your network of contacts. Can you start developing this before you leave by joining groups and clubs? Can you start your new business part-time whilst you are still employed? Can you start to talk to potential clients to find out how interested they may be in you?

If the thought of selling yourself fills you with dread, then seek some training or coaching. Selling is only another form of communication and it is just a matter of confidence and self belief.

INTERVIEWS

Most of us change jobs from time to time and this means attending an interview with a potential new employer. So here are some tips to be at your best at interviews.

Before you attend the interview, find out as much as you can about the company — the internet is a good source of information because company websites often include informative press releases. If they were not provided with your application form, ask the company for their brochures and literature. This helps you to be more informed at the interview and also helps you decide if this is the right company for you.

Make sure that you know exactly where the interview is, how long it will take you to get there and learn about the parking or transport arrangements. There is nothing worse than feeling under time pressure when you are already a bit nervous.

Decide what to wear a couple of days beforehand so that you can check if anything needs cleaning or mending. Wear your favourite business clothes, the ones that you feel smart and comfortable in. Image consultants recommend that you avoid wearing a brand new outfit to an important meeting because you will not have been able to test it out to see whether it is comfortable or fits correctly until the day itself.

Check that your shoes do not need repair. When you want to look your best, you must spend as much time checking all the details as you do on the overall image.

Listen to your favourite upbeat music on the way to the venue. Remind yourself of why you have been offered the interview, recall all the things that you have achieved in your life and remember that you are there because they liked you enough to invite you along.

When you look smart and feel good inside you will act and feel more confident and this will come across to good effect during your interview.

KNOWING

Forgive me for stating the obvious, but then, if it is that obvious, why do so many people seem unaware? It is this, until you know what you want, you cannot get what you want.

Perhaps you are unhappy in your current job but cannot put your finger on the reason. It will certainly involve something that you want [or do not want] so identify what it is. Sometimes it can feel safer not to know, then you reduce the fear of having to make a choice and perhaps getting it wrong. But, sooner or later you will have to make that choice and, the chances are that you will get it right.

Each time that you tell yourself, 'I do not know', you programme your mind not to look for answers to your situation. Instead, you need to think of an empowering question that you can ask yourself to discover your knowing.

If you are unhappy with what you are doing, then you need to do something else. It is totally pointless to keep doing the same thing over and over and expecting a different result.

If you do not know what you want, you probably know what you would hate. Use this as start point to knowing. Very often, your ideal job will turn out to be the exact opposite of the job that would be your worst nightmare.

List everything that you enjoy about your present work.

If you cannot think of a single thing, **why are you still there?**
Even if you think you know nothing, then know this without doubt. Know that you have two choices. You can either do something about your present situation or, you must get honest, stop moaning and get on with it!

LETTERS

Along with your CV, your application letter will be your prospective employer s first impression of you. It must project the right image. Always type the letter unless you are asked to write it by hand. Some companies use a graphologist to analyse what handwriting reveals so it could be a good idea to be forewarned by arranging your own analysis in advance.

Some job advertisements tell you to write to the 'Personnel Manager'. Personally, I always prefer to address it to a person s name. Phone the switchboard and the receptionist will usually give you the name you need.

Keep your letter to one side of one A4 page only. Use pristine white paper and avoid fancy headings or type fonts. Lay the letter out in traditional business letter format. Remember that your aim is to get them to read your CV and invite you for an interview. Put yourself in the position of the interviewer — what will make them choose you?

Carefully study the job advertisement or information pack for the description of the person they are looking for. Pick out one or two key criteria and say how you meet them. If, for example, the advert states, 'attention to detail required', mention how your current or past roles have required you to be responsible for quality control. State briefly why you want the job and the benefits you will bring to the company.

Use a clean envelope and first class post, making sure that you have written the address correctly.

LEADING

Good leaders inspire, rather than making others do things. The leader does not necessarily have to be the boss either, although it does help to be a good leader if you are managing people. A good leader knows the purpose of what is to be achieved and has the ability to communicate this in order to inspire people to work towards the same outcome.

A very important part of successful leading is to 'walk your talk'. Good leaders do not subscribe to the 'do as I tell you, not as I do' school of thought. You need to show others that you are doing what you want them to do. For example, would you take slimming tips from someone who was overweight? When you want people to work in a certain way or do certain things, your actions must be consistent with this desire.

You need to share your vision or goals. If your team does not know what it is aiming for then how can it be expected to be successful? However, having a shared vision does not mean that everyone has to do things in exactly the same way. A good leader will allow others the freedom to explore their own ways to reach the chosen outcome within the confines of the principles you believe in as a leader.

Finally, as the leader, you need to always have one eye on the direction that your team is headed so that if you are going off course, you can quickly redirect activities to bring you back on track.

Never belittle followers. If there were no followers, then every leader would be surplus to requirements!

LIMITS

A recent newspaper survey revealed that almost half of all working women believe that there are barriers in place to prevent their gaining senior roles at work.

Of course, there are prejudices around, but we also hold ourselves back by our limiting beliefs about what is possible for us to achieve.

These brakes apply whether you think you are too old, too young, too fat, too thin, male, female, not qualified enough or even too qualified!

Our limiting beliefs offer us excuses for not achieving what we say we really want. They allow us to blame something or someone else for our lack of progress. The trouble is, that when you spend all your time focusing on what you think you cannot do, you will miss the opportunities that are available to you.

If you then allow other people s views about limits to affect you as well, you really will be tying yourself up in knots! People sometimes tell you that you will not be able to achieve something because, if you start to change, it could make them feel uncomfortable about their own achievements.

Another aspect of the survey results is that we may be all saying we want senior roles at work just because we think that we should want such goals. Deep down, this may conflict with some of your core values with the result that you inadvertently sabotage your own success.

For example, you may believe that in order to gain a promotion you must work long hours. This could result in conflict if one of your core values is to relax and have fun. Therefore, you will knuckle down and work hard for a while but every so often, you will 'flip out' and take unplanned time off work or even disappear for a three-hour lunch, which your boss will disapprove of.

It is important to decide what you really want in your career. Ban your limiting self-beliefs and then you will have no trouble committing to do whatever it takes to achieve it.

LISTENING
We listen in many different ways

When someone is telling you about something you have heard before, you might be thinking, 'Not this story again' or, you might be thinking 'Let me tell them about my experience'. Either way, you are not really listening because you are busy chatting away to yourself instead.

There are other ways of listening too. Have you ever been talking in a group at a party when someone outside of the group mentions either your name or something that interests you? You then join this new conversation? That is selective listening — you are always checking to see that you are not missing anything that is going on around you. That is OK in some situations, but not in others (like a coaching environment) where you need to give the other person 100% of your attention.

So, what kind of listening do coaches use? Empathic listening. This completely and deliberately closes down any inner dialogue to really listen to what the other person is saying. By removing all distractions, you can see things from their perspective. You are able to repeat what they said — possibly even using the same words.

Develop your listening skills with a friend. Ask them to talk to you about something that really interests them for a minute or so. Listen to them without nodding, shaking your head, interrupting, muttering, grunting or making any other sound of approval or disapproval. You may well be surprised at how difficult this is to do, but how easy it is to learn. After all, there is a reason why you have two ears but only one mouth!

LUCK

It is said that luck, like opportunity, favours the prepared mind. A wealthy person once said, 'the more I work to turn an idea into reality, the luckier I become'.

Luck does not just happen. You have to make it happen by running your life so that it can come in whenever you need it. Luck does not mean having something fall into your lap. You may be on a 'high' for a little while, but true lasting enjoyment comes from achievement that you have created or earned through your actions.

Some people may seem lucky at work. It could be that they have realised that doing a good job simply creates a fair reward. They know that they have to do, and be seen to be doing, an excellent job in order to attract an excellent result.

Lack of apparent luck may be the outcome of allowing familiarity to breed contempt, especially when you have been in your job for a long time. Approach each task as if it is the first time that you have done it for a new prospective employer or target. Do it with passion and energy. Do it to the absolute best of your ability. You may be pleasantly surprised at how 'lucky' you become.

When you keep your mind on excellence in everything that you say, think and do, it will eventually become your normal way of working and your normal way of life. Plan your life around giving equal importance to what you can do for others . 'Ask not what others can do for you, but what you can do for them', then do it with enthusiasm and excellence. Your good luck will follow as a positive side effect.

MARKETING

So what is marketing? It is all about satisfying customers. That involves finding out what they want and then offering it!

Firstly, identify your customers. Everyone you deal with is your customer, whether it is your boss, colleagues, external customers or suppliers. All relationships are exchanges of value — whether it is selling something or supplying information to your boss.

So how do you find out what your customers want? Ask them! In marketing terms, this is called researching your target market. Finding out what your customers want, rather than assuming you know, may save you a lot of work. For example, your boss may always want certain information to be on their desk every Monday morning, but may not require it to be beautifully typed.

When you have found out what your customers want, you can set about altering your services to meet their needs. For example, are your reports in the easiest format for them to read and understand? Are you giving positive messages? Are you always ready to try new ideas or, can you always see reasons why new ideas will not work? Are you available when they need you? Are you really delivering value for money? If you satisfy your customers, you will find it easy to get what you want in life.

MEETINGS

Do you seem to spend most of your working day in meetings? With busier schedules, meetings have become a necessary part of business today. However, there are ways to ensure that the time you spend in meetings is productive.

If you are managing the meeting, identify your objectives and desired results, then circulate an agenda outlining those objectives to all participants in advance. If you regularly attend meetings without agendas, it is possible that they have no definite objectives and maybe you should query why you attend!

During the meeting, someone should be appointed to keep discussions on track. They should be assertive enough to pull participants back to the agenda points if necessary. Other matters can always be saved until the end or scheduled for a future meeting. Someone else should be taking note of the main points agreed - the minutes - and any action points to be completed after the meeting. Action points should have an agreed deadline for completion and a note of who is to make it happen. Circulate the minutes as soon after the meeting as possible while it is still fresh in everyone s minds.

If you run all your meetings in this way, you should spend less time in them!

MISTAKES

We all make mistakes from time to time. All successful people will tell you that if you want to double your successes, you must first double your number of mistakes! No one is immune, but the secret of publicly recovering from your mistakes is to manage their publicity.

Look at some famous examples of mistakes having been made, such as Bill Clinton and Monica Lewinsky. The way they managed the publicity of the mistake affected their reputations. So, if you find yourself having made a serious mistake, take a leaf out of the PR book.

Be the one to tell people — do not try to cover it up in the hope that it will not be noticed — people respect honesty. Do not try to frame someone else. Apologise for the error and either suggest ways to put things right or actually start the process of correcting things. This shows that you are proactive and willing to take responsibility.

If others contributed to the mistake, take more control over your own projects in the future and take the time now to build stronger relationships with people that you rely on to help you.

To improve your image, publicise your future successes to reduce the negative memory of the past error.

Finally, if you discover someone else s mistake, this also takes careful managing. Remember, they may discover a fault of yours one day, so bear this in mind when you decide how to publicise their error!

MOTIVATION

Do you ever find it hard to motivate yourself? Perhaps you start a project but then run out of steam and give up on it? Or perhaps you cannot even get yourself to start a project like looking for a new job? These tips may help you.

Firstly, you need to know WHY you want to take the action. If you have a strong enough reason to do something then you will find it easier to work out how to do it. Think about any major decision you have ever made; it was probably because you had a strong reason to make it.

Generally, there are two main reasons why people get motivated to take action. Those reasons are either to gain pleasure or to avoid pain. Which one is it for you? It will not always be the same reason in every area of your life.

If you keep starting projects but never finish them, you are likely to be trying to avoid some sort of pain. Unfortunately, with this motivation strategy, when you get far enough away from the imagined pain, you become comfortable again and often stop taking action when this happens. You need to keep reminding yourself of the negative consequences of stopping — It is using the stick end of the 'carrot & stick' approach to keep you moving!

If, on the other hand, you have a project that you have never started, it is likely that there is no pain associated with not achieving it and little pleasure to be gained. This could be because it is a project that is not important to you, or because you have not created a compelling enough reason for you to want to take action. To get yourself motivated in this instance you need to adopt the carrot approach and imagine the pleasures and rewards of successfully completing the project.

After all, to a donkey, a carrot is just a pointed orange stick. The difference is the end to which it is applied!

MOMENTUM

Some of your personal goals may seem very large and possibly a long way off. So how do you keep momentum going whilst you are on your journey?

Firstly, you must take time every day to check your progress on your path towards your goals. Some people like the discipline of keeping a journal so that they can look back and see how much they have achieved.

Secondly, you have to control what you focus your attention on. If you concentrate on the fact that your goal is still a long way away, you are more likely to feel like giving up. You must acknowledge what you have achieved and congratulate yourself on how much closer you are to your ultimate goal. Say how good you feel about this in your journal. It also helps you to notice the days that slip by when you have not moved towards your goals too - but do not beat yourself up over this, just use it as a spur to avoid further backsliding.

Another important thing to keep in mind is that working towards goals is a journey where you learn and enjoy a lot on the way. It is not all about the final destination. Otherwise, you will always have your life on hold waiting 'until'   until you achieve the fit body, until you own that expensive car, or whatever else you want in life.

Count your blessings every day. Remember all the people who are dear to you and all the great things and experiences that you have in your life.

Developing an attitude of gratitude can help you sustain your momentum.

NEGOTIATING

Getting what you want can be simple when you know the secrets used by successful negotiators. So, whether you want to ask for a pay rise, to go on a training course, or for time off, use this process to help you on your way to success.

Firstly, define what you want — what is your ideal outcome and what result could you be happy with if you had to bargain? Next, put yourself into the other person s position. What objections may they have to your request? What would convince them that your request should be met? What is the benefit to them in your request? Identify these important points then think of how you would overcome any objections and reassure the other party that compliance with your request will benefit them too.

Before your meeting, prepare yourself. You may find it helpful to write down what you want with all your arguments to support your request. Then you are not sidetracked.

During the meeting, remember that everyone is entitled to their own opinion and should be allowed to express it. Just because you do not agree with each other, it does not mean that one of you is wrong. This is worth remembering from both sides of the negotiating table!

Throughout your negotiation, try to aim for a solution that makes both of you happy. If you end up with a solution that one of you feels unhappy with, then this will sour the relationship for future negotiations.

Remember, when negotiating, aim for a win-win situation so that you both feel that you have gained from the agreement!

NERVES

How can you control the inevitable nerves that you will feel before an interview?

Firstly, it is important to acknowledge that nerves are your body s natural preparation for action — it is the fight or flight preparation that cuts in when you know that you are about to do something outside your normal comfort zone. In fact, without any of these nerves, then you probably would not perform at all well. Many famous people suffer from nerves or stage fright but they still deliver on their talent. Therefore, feeling nervous does not prevent you from doing something.

Secondly, find a way to store up confident feelings that you can recall in an instant. Perhaps a certain piece of music makes you want to smile, dance and sing at the top of your voice? I have made a tape of all my favourite music to play in my car on the way to important meetings. You may prefer to recall a memory of an event that makes you feel confident. Practice recalling it at will and seeing a mental picture of that memory in full colour with surround sound — just like a movie — until you get all the confident feelings back.

On the way to the interview, play the music or recall the memory in your head and focus on the good feelings. Imagine that you are an actor and you have to perform as if you are confident — stand tall, breathe deeply and smile, just like a confident person would — and before you know it you will actually be feeling confident.

This is one the few times in life where it is quite acceptable to fake it 'til you make it!

NETWORKING

Have you noticed how some people always seem to hear about the best jobs, bargains or parties? Would you like to know how they do it? Their secret is being good at networking. So what is networking and can anyone do it?

Networking is about enhancing something we do naturally — sharing information with people. It is a skill we can all improve and, if you follow the golden rule of networking, you need never feel awkward about telling other people about what you want.

The golden rule is that you should consider networking as a way of meeting new people. Networking is not selling. It is about finding out more about others' unique skills so that you can use this information when you need to. It is a bit like window-shopping — you know where you can get what you want when you want it.

People love to help others solve their problems. Often these solutions can be in the form of recommending someone or something that will help. Most of us prefer to recommend others that we know and like. Therefore, the more people who know and like you, the more chance you will be recommended as the solution!

So how do you network? Become aware of the opportunities that are all around you. Start with your friends. If you are looking for a new job or more party invitations, let them know.

When you go to events, meetings and parties, talk to people you have not met before. Ask them about themselves because this will endear them to you and encourage them to ask about you. Get some business cards printed so that you can give new friends your contact details.

Set yourself targets of the number of people you want to meet every month and make sure you do it.

NO

It is not nice to hear 'No'. Yet, adults quite readily accept the word as a final decision, but children do not. If you listen to children, they will ask and ask until they get what they want — and they can be very creative with their methods of asking too!

Research has found that, by the age of 18, we will have heard the word more than 20,000 times. I wonder if that has anything to do with our acceptance of rejection as we get older? We accept others decisions with a shrug and a 'that s life' attitude.

If you think about anyone who has made a great achievement in life — whether they are inventors or pop stars — they have learnt not to accept 'No' as a final decision. They have kept on trying until they have achieved what they wanted — just as children do.

So, perhaps the secret is to be more childlike when we are trying to achieve something. That is not to say that you should do the same thing over and over again — or throw an infantile tantrum. Just do something slightly differently until you achieve what you want. It took over 70,000 experiments before the electric light bulb was invented — just think where we would be if Thomas Edison had given up before he d got what he wanted? Henry Ford was told 'No' when he first introduced the notion of mass production. Col. Sanders was no stranger to the word - it was two years of daily endeavour before he found a restaurant willing to buy his secret fried chicken recipe.

At a school speech day, wartime prime minister Winston Churchill said just six words - 'Never, never, never, never give up'. Remember this the next time you hear 'No'.

OBJECTIONS

Every sales person knows that buyers will always have objections that need to be overcome. Whether the objection is to do with price or anything else, the seller will always have to try to make the buyer see the positive aspects of their previous doubt. Think about when you are buying an expensive item, you will always have a couple of doubts that need to be addressed before you make the final decision to buy.

It is exactly the same when you are selling yourself for a job. The interviewer has choices of people to appoint and will have preferences and doubts about people for different reasons. In order to be successful in getting the job, the interviewer needs to feel happy that they have made the best choice.

An excellent way to prepare to sell yourself is to think of all the possible objections that might be levied against you. Perhaps you are worried that employers will think you are too old or too young or, that you have spent too long or not long enough in your current job. Make a list of all the possible objections you can think of.

Next taking each objection, think about how you could reframe it positively to represent it as one of your strengths. For example, if you are concerned that a possible objection may be that you are too old. You can reframe this by the fact that experience comes only with time and you have combined this seniority by keeping up to date with the latest issues that affect your industry (make sure that you have!)

Prepare this list of objections and reframes before you start job hunting. They will help you deliver the results that you want.

OBJECTIVES

Objectives are closely related to goals, but they are not the same.

There is an old saying that is still true. It goes like this, 'When you are up to your backside in alligators, it is difficult to remember that the original objective was to drain the pool'.

When you begin any task with a clean sheet, you will have a clear idea of the ultimate result or objective. As you get into the job you will be tempted by trivia, distractions and other activities that contribute absolutely nothing to the outcome or results of your project or assignment. They can be as dangerous as a shrinking pool full of hungry alligators.

When a possible diversion crops up, remind yourself of your single prime objective. If this new idea allows you to take a short cut that will move you closer to the original aim, then use it. If it does not, then it may still be valuable another time so simply write it down in your diary so that you can return to it when the job in hand is finished.

Your diary should not just be used for dates and appointments. Choose one that has big pages so that you can use it as a journal for great ideas as they occur...

Richard Branson is famous for many reasons. His staff know that he usually carries an A4 hardback notebook and writes frequent brief notes to himself. When an idea has been written you can forget it while you focus on your objective. Then you can return to it at a more convenient time when you can evaluate the idea in a cool, clear and collected manner.

OVERLOAD

We all feel overloaded from time to time, either from having too much to do or from having too many demands on our time. A common feeling of overload is of being out of control and trapped in a cycle where there is no escape.

So, you have too much to do. It may seem odd, but I am going to suggest that you do something else! Write down everything that you must do, together with deadlines and expectations you have of the tasks. Take this list to a boss or impartial friend and look through it together. Is there anything that can be delayed, deleted or delegated? Are there things where expectations can be lowered? If you feel uncomfortable at the thought of delegating things to others, you need to consider why you are scared of letting go and reluctant to trust others.

Prepare a list of essential tasks. Negotiate any deadline extensions that you need. There are few things that cannot be extended, but you may need some help with assertiveness skills to enable you to feel happy when negotiating. Whilst on the subject of assertiveness, practice saying NO to things that are not important and that cause you overload. This will seem hard at first but by always saying, 'yes' you have been training people to dump on you without notice.

Finally, give yourself time off — this seems impossible when you have loads to do, but a break will bring you back refreshed. Take a lunch break, go to the gym or do whatever else you have been putting off 'until I've got straight'. If you are kind to yourself, you will be able to do more anyway. If you are struggling with this idea, think about whether you would make someone you love work without breaks - then treat yourself with the same kindness.

PARTIES

Some people love them, they enjoy the planning, they look forward to the event for ages and spend months afterwards talking about it. For others, attending any party can be an ordeal, with the notorious office party at the top of the list. If you have run out of excuses and really cannot avoid attending a party, it pays to work out your plan of attack beforehand.

Firstly, find out who is going and see if you can arrange to arrive with a friend. This ensures you have someone to touch base with during the evening if you become bored with strangers' small talk. Next, be clear about the expected dress code and plan to wear something you feel really comfortable and confident in. This is not the time to try out a new image that could make you feel awkward. Have something to eat before you leave home then, if you are tempted to calm your nerves with a couple of drinks, they will not land on an empty stomach!

When you get to the party, start off with the people you know. With strangers, practise the rapport skill of matching their body language — this helps to get over initial lack of things to say. Get them to introduce you to other people they know. Ask them lots of questions about themselves and you will have no worries about making conversation - but avoid being nosey or impolite. See the party as an opportunity to find out about lots of new people — you could even have a competition with a friend to see how many you can each meet during the party.

Alternate alcoholic drinks with soft ones so that you can remember who you speak to during the evening. It is worth keeping in mind that, despite how confident other people seem, they could be as nervous as you.

PERSPECTIVE

Even if you have never been for a helicopter ride, you will be able to relate to this story.

You may be stuck in a motorway traffic jam. All you can see is the back bumper of the lorry in front of you. It seems that the other lanes of traffic are moving faster than yours, but you cannot safely move over. If it was possible to rise a hundred feet over the road, you would be able to see that the other lanes are just as jammed for the next few miles.

Go up to a thousand feet and you will see even further ahead. You will see that there are two exit roads before the traffic accident that is blocking the motorway. Double your height again, and you will notice that the first exit leads to another congestion situation but that the second one is clear.

When you are closely involved with a job, you may hit a problem, difficulty or delay. Instead of immediately becoming frustrated and upset, take some time out. Do something different for a few moments. As soon as you distance yourself a little, you will get a new perspective on the issue. You may well see an alternative way to get you to where you want to be.

Think of a fly that beats itself to death by repeatedly hitting its head against a closed window in desperation to get out. If it could take a different perspective it would probably see the open door next to the window and fly easily into freedom.

A famous poet once said that 'distance lends enchantment to the view'. He must have had a life coach!

PERSUASION

We all need to write to people to persuade them to do something we want from time to time. Whether you are writing a memo to your boss or a press release in the hope of getting a story about your company published, you can increase your chances of success.

Firstly, decide on your objective for your writing. Next, think about your readers. Who are they? How much do they know about your topic? Will you need to give them some background information or explain any jargon? Most importantly, 'what is in it for them' to read and take the action you are requesting?

There must always be a benefit for your readers

You have your objective and have thought about the situation from your reader s point of view. When you start writing, imagine you are having a conversation with them and use the kinds of words you would use when you speak to people. In conversation you might say, 'I am looking forward to my holiday', so do not write 'I am eagerly anticipating my annual vacation'. Avoid attempting to write for effect, as this will cloud the clarity of your message. Never use a long or obscure word if a short and simple one will do.

Think of an attention grabbing heading that you can use that relates to the subject of your writing. Put your most important point in the first paragraph in case they stop reading for any reason. Keep to the facts, avoid opinions and resist the temptation to introduce needless comments.

Do not be afraid to ask for what you want — making sure your reader knows clearly what it is that you want them to do.

POLITICS
Office politics happen. In all types of organisations, where groups of people work together, there will always be sides taken and alliances formed. For various reasons this can create disharmony. We do not always work with everyone we naturally like, we may find ourselves with conflicting loyalties and, of course, we are not always confident and assertive enough to tell the truth.

Think you cannot avoid getting caught up in it? Or maybe you enjoy the excitement of getting involved? It is always best to find another way to get your kicks, preferably outside of work and keep political neutrality in any battle that is not your own. You never know when the situation may change and your allegiances and behaviour could backfire on you. Find ways to minimise the impact that office politics have on you and your life at work.

Do not get sucked into battles that are none of your business. Make your own decisions and form your own opinions about a situation. Do not be afraid to stand on your own. Other people will attempt to draw you towards their side of a dispute — they are simply playing the 'safety in numbers' game. Do not be flattered by being included. If you are not directly affected by what is going on, do not join in just to relieve the regular routine of work.

Learn to be assertive and give honest, respectful, feedback to others. Dare to behave differently from the majority and you will find that others will react in a different way to you.

You may find that you suffer gossip withdrawal symptoms, but you will gain respect from all sides. When you are true to your values and valid beliefs, there is never any need for you to play office power games.

PRESENTATIONS

Some people fear making presentations more than they fear dying! But it is really easy to overcome those fears.

It is all about mastering your state of mind so that you can relax and make a good presentation. It is helpful to create a strong anchor to good feelings that you want to feel when you are presenting, for example, confidence. It is very easy to do this. It works in the same way that certain things trigger off memories and feelings.

Here is how to do it. Decide upon the feeling you would like, say it is calmness. Then remember a time when you felt really calm. Make a vivid picture of the memory in your mind and remember the sounds and feelings that went with it. When you feel you are at the peak of the calm feelings, do something unique like squeeze your hand into a fist. This creates an anchor for those good feelings. You can stack several good feelings on top of each other by doing the same exercise over and over again. This makes the anchor even stronger. Then anytime you want to feel good, just make a fist!

PRIORITIES

If you have ever read anything about time management, you will be familiar with the idea of prioritising the tasks that you have to do, by putting the most important ones first and listing the others in order of urgency.

Of course, there is no such thing as time management. It is just another term for what is really self management. We all have the same number of hours in the day, it is how we each manage our lives that determines what results and happiness we achieve in those hours.

Next weekend, or even during a holiday if you have one due soon, imagine how great it would be if you could maintain your relaxed state when you return to work. You will feel better, you will work better and you will get more done in less time. Here is a useful way to work towards this.

Instead of prioritising tasks, focus on your personal priorities. Think about health, diet, happiness, sleep patterns, quality family time, relaxation, leisure interests and so on. You must make the time to look after yourself in all these areas and any others that you can come up with as being important to you.

Overdue tasks often become urgent. Urgency creates stress and stress is the enemy of organisation so that even urgent jobs fall even further behind. When you fail to take time for yourself, you could create a truly urgent situation in the form of illness. What impact will that have on all those tasks that were urgent yesterday?

Plan time for yourself. Use it for yourself. Then you will maintain your mind and body in a great working condition to tackle any challenges before they turn into crises.

PROCRASTINATION
We all procrastinate over certain tasks. It maybe a task at work, such as writing a report, or a task at home such as clearing out cupboards. And, isn t it amazing how creative we can be about reasons why we have not done something? So, if we can take time to create excuses, we can take time to actually do the task instead.

Firstly, ask yourself what is stopping you starting the task? It maybe that it seems too big, you may be worried about failing - or succeeding on the false belief that success will add more pressure and responsibilities.

If the task seems too big to tackle, try this advice from Stephen Covey, a time management expert: 'By the inch it is a cinch, by the yard it is hard.' Break the task into small chunks and then tackle one chunk at a time. Before long, you will have made a significant impact on the task. Another way of 'chunking down' is to commit to spend a defined time on each segment or element, and then after that you are free.

If you think you are procrastinating because you are scared, try acting as if you are not. Pretend to be someone who is not scared and who can do the task. Then take action, no matter how cautious you may feel, and you reduce the fear.

Something I learned from another time management expert, Edmund Bliss, is not to reward procrastination but reward action. So the next time you think, 'I ll just have a coffee and then I ll start ' stop yourself right there! Do the task first and then reward yourself. This will change the link between inactivity and reward in your brain. The only place where reward comes before work is in the dictionary!

The only cure for procrastination is action. Do not wait to feel better until you tackle that job. Take action now and you will be amazed at how much better you feel.

Remember this mantra. **'Do it. Do it now.'**

PROJECTS

There are many ways to manage projects, but my suggestion for stress-free project management is as follows:

Make sure you know all of the deadlines and outcomes that you are expected to achieve. In addition, it helps to know who will be affected or involved in the project.

Get everyone working on the project together to brainstorm everything that has to happen, by whom, and by when. Also, plan in promotional activities like newsletters and memos keeping others up-to-date with progress. This is especially important if the project will affect many different people within the organisation.

Create a centrally controlled document — you can buy specialist project management software — but a spreadsheet would probably do the job just as well. Sometimes called a Critical Path Analysis, the document should show all activities and action points in the sequence that they must follow. It allows you to forecast the knock-on effects of any delays in start and finish times.

This should be circulated and regularly updated (nominate one person to do this) with progress reports to everyone responsible for action and to managers affected by the project. This is particularly useful if anyone becomes ill or takes a holiday.

Set up regular meetings with the people working on the project. These meetings should be centred on action points with an opportunity for people to get to know each other better and raise any questions that may have occurred to them.

If you are in charge of the project, make sure you lead your team by example. Meet deadlines that you have agreed, keep documents up-to-date and maintain good communication with team members.

When the project has been completed, remember to follow up and thank everyone involved and to publicise the success of the project to others outside of the team.

PROMOTION

When we find a job and a company we like, most of us are content to work hard as long as there is the prospect of future promotion. These tips may help you to move promotion from mere wishes towards distinct possibilities.

Firstly, you need to have an idea of the role you would like. This may be in a similar area to the work you are currently doing, or in a completely new one. Find out as much about the role as possible so that you can be sure that you really do want it, before you go to the effort of trying for it!

Become an observer and watch how people who are currently doing that job behave. For example, in meetings — do they contribute actively? Also, notice things like how they respond to requests for information, what their timekeeping is like and how tidy their work area is. You could even ask to take them out for lunch in return for picking their brains about how they are successful in their jobs.

Speak to your boss, or the manager of the other department, to find out what they expect from people doing the role you have identified. You need to build up an idea of how you would need to behave at work in order to be seriously considered for promotion to that role. You will also be able to find out what sort of qualities they would be looking for you to demonstrate in order to consider you for promotion.

Practise some of this desired behaviour in your current role. This is particularly important if there are big differences between what is required for promotion and your current attitude at work.

QUESTIONS

You know how to control interview nerves and how to look your best. Here are some tips to prepare yourself for interview questions.

As well as doing some pre-interview research on your potential employer, it is useful to find out about the industry in general. Who are the major companies involved? Who is the market leader? What kind of customers does your prospective employer have? What forces outside of the company may affect the way that they do business in the future? Your awareness of these things will impress your interviewer and show your true interest in joining the company.

Think about your skills and capabilities. A favourite question is to ask you about your strengths and weaknesses? Ask your friends and colleagues for their opinions as we usually tend to under-estimate our own strengths. How could you match your strengths to what the company needs? This is known as benefit selling.

Look again at your CV and application letter. What did you write about, particularly concerning your achievements? The interviewer is likely to ask you questions about these. Can you remember all the facts and figures or do you need to do a bit of revision? Prepare to talk about what you learnt about yourself whilst making these achievements. Also, be prepared to point out how you would have improved things if you had the benefit of hindsight. Interviewers seem to like asking candidates to state their worst points!

Armed with the information you have researched about the company and your arguments about how you would be the best candidate, you will be in an excellent position to feel confident and portray yourself to your best abilities.

QUITTING

How do you treat your employer when you decide to leave?

Firstly, get your new job offer in writing before you take any further action. Once you have this, check the terms and conditions of your existing contract — how long is your notice period? Then you can inform your new employer when you will be free to start employment with them.

When you are ready to quit, stop for a moment and think about the future. Resist the temptation to resign in a flourish of 'you can stick your job' — you never know when you may need a reference or you may meet colleagues again in the future.

Be as professional as you are with your new company. Even if your current employers have treated you badly, there is no need for you to behave in the same way.

Think about how you like bad news to be delivered. No matter what you think of your manager, your resignation will be bad news for them because, if nothing else, they will have the hassle of replacing you. Therefore, deliver the news to your manager in person and make sure they hear the news from you first, rather than through the office grapevine.

Once you have had a discussion, you can confirm your resignation in writing later. Remember that this letter may remain on file so find something positive to say about your employment experience with them — even if it is something small.

Whilst working your notice period, resist the temptation to brag about how great your new company is going to be and how awful this job is — your colleagues may not agree with you. Also, keep doing your job as if you were not leaving — you want to leave behind a good impression wherever you have been.

Just remember this, 'never foul an empty nest in case you need to use it again'. It is always better to leave with friends behind you, rather than needlessly creating enemies to satisfy your ego.

RAPPORT

The ability to get on well with people is a vital skill in business. Sometimes it can take a while to get to know someone well enough that you can both relax easily. However, there are some ways to speed up the process of 'getting to know each other' and these techniques are known as building rapport.

So, what is rapport? Well, when you are friends with someone, you feel very relaxed in their company and can talk about virtually anything. This is because you are naturally 'in rapport' with people you like. Rapport between two people is about each being like the other. The old saying about opposites attracting is false. We naturally gravitate towards people who are like us or have attributes that we would like to have ourselves.

So how can you turn something natural and unconscious into a tool that you can use in the workplace? Rapport is about matching similarities. The easiest way to start creating rapport is to match the other person's body language; the way they sit, how they cross their legs and the gestures they use. The next time you have the opportunity to 'people watch' notice how similarly groups of people move and behave.

You can increase the similarities between you and another person by matching their body language, laughing when they laugh, sitting forward when they do, speaking at similar pace, tone and volume. But you must be subtle - you do not want them to notice and think you are trying to be funny.

The best way is to practice on one thing at a time, such as facial expressions. If you are building rapport on the phone you can also match the words the other person uses - this is a very useful tool when you are selling an idea to someone.

Rapport building is a really useful skill to learn. It is great for reducing any awkward period when you first meet someone and it is wonderful for developing relationships as it really helps with communication.

Try it yourself for 30 days and notice the improvements you have in all your dealings with other people.

REDUNDANCY

Redundancy is something that can happen to anyone at any time. It is usually beyond their control. However, you CAN control your reactions if it happens to you.

This begins by acknowledging that losing your job will create similar feelings to any other kind of loss or bereavement. You will cycle through a menu of emotions ranging from shock, disbelief, anger, hurt, betrayal, fear, guilt and sometimes even wanting revenge. You may even experience several of these feelings at the same time.

However, despite all of these negative feelings, remember that positive change comes out of chaos. For example, farmers burn stubble in fields in order for new growth to come through. Each autumn the leaves fall from trees to allow the new buds to appear.

This can be an ideal opportunity to make decisions about your future. If you have some redundancy money, you have the luxury of some time to think about what you really want to do. Do not to sit back for several months and wait until the money runs out before you decide to look for other work.

Revisit [or create] your life s goals and decide whether you want to retrain, stay in the same industry, take time out to travel, or start your own business. If you do decide to go travelling, remember you do have to come back one day and find a job, so before you leave, plan what you will do on your return.

If you aim to launch your own business, get some impartial advice, particularly if you have received a large redundancy payout. Make sure that you invest or spend your money wisely.

Look upon this enforced change as a new cycle of your life. If you find yourself feeling extreme levels of grief at your loss, consider the good things in your life and seek other non-work related ways to direct your energies.

Above all, the way to cope with any situation is to take control. You may feel like a victim - who has things happen to them, but that awareness can spur you to a determination to become a victor - who makes things happen.

REJECTION

Keeping your confidence, enthusiasm and motivation high can be a challenge when you receive rejection. No one likes rejection, but there are ways you can train yourself to reduce the negative feelings and even welcome them!

The main danger is that one rejection can create a fear about more. If you allow this fear to take hold, you may even give up trying to reach your goals. This is because the fear presents too much to risk. However, most successful people in the world have learned to cope with rejection and risk. Very few have experienced a major success with their first attempt. More than 1000 theatrical agents and movie moguls turned down Sylvester Stallone before he got his break in Rocky.

You must retain a powerful thought about exactly what you want. Then you have to vividly imagine achieving it. Remember when you were younger and you wanted something, you would imagine wearing it or playing with it? Well do the same now. Imagine what you will look like and how you will feel when you have reached your goal. Make this goal so compelling that you feel that you cannot wait to have it.

Next, you have to take on this firm new belief - there is no failure, there are only results. Everything that you do produces a result. Therefore, if you do something and it does not produce the result you wanted, do something different and get another result.

There are no limits to the times that you can do something different. You have not tried every way until you have reached your goal. Ask yourself this question, 'If I knew that I could not fail, what would I do today?' So now, when you experience rejection, you can welcome that result as a message that you need to do something different!

RELATIONSHIPS

There may be many reasons why any relationship is seen as difficult. However, to change things for the better you have to change yourself. You can try forever to change other people, without much success. But it is much quicker and easier to change the way that you react and feel. Changing your reaction is often all that is needed to break the pattern of past dealings with each other.

Examine the relationship from the other person s point of view. What do you think is their positive intention of their behaviour? It may be that they feel insecure or threatened and behave in this way to make themselves feel better.

To get another perspective on the relationship, try taking an impartial observer s viewpoint, looking at both of you. Notice whether there is anything that you can do to improve the relationship and anything that you can stop doing that creates a bad reaction or result.

If you still find the other person difficult to deal with, it may just be worth accepting that there are many different ways to view the world and just because you disagree, it does not mean that either of you are wrong.

Of course, you can always terminate a relationship but, never think about terminating a relation!

RELEASE

There are claims that stress is one of the biggest causes of workplace absence. Stress can be a result of working long hours, worry, anger, frustration or even boredom. In Britain, we work longer hours and have more heart disease than many of our European neighbours, so we really should take some action to release the effects of stress.

Most of us have used alcohol, food, nicotine or television to distract us from a stressful situation. However, some television shows actually raise blood pressure and we also know that alcohol may numb stress temporarily, but with a hangover, the situation will seem twice as bad!

So, investigate some more positive ways of releasing stress and relaxing. For example, find time to learn a new skill that totally absorbs you while you are learning. When you become absorbed in something, you stop thinking about things that cause you stress.

If you do not trust yourself to get absorbed by yourself then pay for lessons — when you are paying, you are more likely to get involved! If you think you do not have time to do this, then look at the balance in your life currently.

You are your biggest asset and assets need looking after. If you managed an athlete, would you make him or her compete every day without rest and recuperation? So why do not you give yourself the same opportunities?

Take time out and you will come back to your work refreshed and ready to take on whatever awaits you.

RESOLUTIONS

At new year, or on your birthday, it is common to look back on what you have achieved and look forward to what you want to achieve in the months ahead. Often we are full of hope when setting resolutions but quickly find that they are forgotten in the process of getting on with living.

So how can you ensure that you will maintain progress towards your resolutions? Firstly, remember that THE PAST DOES NOT EQUAL THE FUTURE. Therefore, if you have not been successful in achieving something in the past it does not mean that you cannot do it in the future. It just means that whatever you tried last time did not give you the outcome you wanted.

How long did it take you to learn how to walk? Did you give up the first time you fell over? **Exactly!** This kind of determination is what you need to ensure that your new resolutions are not forgotten!

People who set goals are far more likely to be successful than those who just let things happen. The secret is to know what you want, take action, be aware of the result you get and, if you do not like the result, do something different until you get the result you want. If it feels tough, remember the learning to walk metaphor and keep going!

ROLES

Everyone has different roles in life. You may, at different times, be an accountant when you balance your personal budget, a parent or spouse, brother or sister, worker, hobbyist, holidaymaker, traveller and so on.

Take a few minutes to write down as many roles as you can think of. Then, instead of thinking about which ones you enjoy the most, consider how much satisfaction you get from each of them. Award yourself 10 points, and a pat on the back, for any that you are totally satisfied with. Award a lower score for less satisfaction.

What would need to be different for each lower score to be raised? What actions will you take, starting today, to raise those scores?

Notice that word 'you'. You should not attempt to change other people to raise your own score, but you can change your own outlook, viewpoint or approach. This matters because, when you are less than 100% satisfied with any of your roles, you will not play the part to the best of your ability and this is not being fair to yourself.

Unlike an actor who may have to audition for a role and then be offered the part, many of your roles will be thrust upon you, so you owe it to yourself and your significant others to make the best job that you can of each of them. An actor can pretend for the duration of their performance. You do not have that luxury. You must replace pretence with sincerity. Sincerity comes easier when you have the satisfaction of knowing that you play your roles for life to the best of your ability.

ROMANCE

We spend more waking hours at work than anywhere else, so it stands to reason that your workplace is one of the most likely places to meet your partner. So, if this happens to you, how will you manage your relationship whilst maintaining your professional standing and keeping the respect of your colleagues?

When your relationship first starts, it is probably a good idea to be as discreet as possible until you know whether or not it is serious. There is little point everyone knowing if it only lasts a few days. Once you have decided that it is time to tell other people, tell your immediate colleagues rather than let them find out through the grapevine — especially if one of you is the boss.

You need to decide how you will behave at work towards each other and how much of your private life you will bring to work. For example, how will you behave if you have had a row?

Be aware that you might receive mixed reactions to the news of your relationship. Some of your colleagues might feel that you cannot be friends if you are also going home with the boss at night. You may need to assess how your future promotion prospects could be affected. You may have to be prepared to work twice as hard to prove you deserve any future advancement.

If the worst happens and you break up, if you are going to continue working together then you will have to behave correctly to each other. However, looking on the bright side, if your relationship continues you will be one of the few people who actually spend more time with their partners than their colleagues!

SALARIES

Are you feeling financially worse off? Want to negotiate a salary increase? Be prepared so that you stand a better chance of getting a better deal for yourself.

You will need to book a meeting with your manager to discuss your performance and pay. Before the meeting, have a look at the objectives that you agreed with your manager at your last review or appraisal. How have you performed against your targets? Where can you show your extra contribution to the organisation?

Read your company newsletters and get a feel for how the company is doing — not all companies are suffering in the current economic climate. Also, look at job adverts from your company s competitors — what do they pay for similar types of jobs that you are doing?

Prepare the terms that you want to negotiate, including the ideal package and the lowest increase that you would settle for. Also, think about any other 'perks' you would like to ask for — for example sponsorship on a training course.

You need to be assertive by clearly stating your request and the reasons to support it, but also be willing to listen to your manager s comments. At all costs, avoid being aggressive and confrontational. Never threaten to leave if you do not get what you want — no one likes to be blackmailed and you may find that your manager calls your bluff!

Do this preparation and approach your manager correctly and you will stand more chance of being successful. However, sometimes your manager will still refuse your first request. If this happens, find out why and be prepared to negotiate for a situation where you both feel happy. At the very least, agree a time in the near future when you can discuss this again.

After your meeting, if you feel that you really are not paid enough, you can always apply for some of the jobs you used in your research!

SATISFACTION

A recent magazine survey suggested that over 60% of people are satisfied by their work. But what do you do if you are one of the other 40%?

List everything that is important to you in a work environment. Some examples may be; recognition, creativity, freedom, autonomy and so on.

The next step is to look at your list and find at least three examples of times when each of your values has been met at work. For example, if recognition is important to you, you may have received this from customers, colleagues or bosses. Recognition can be in any form such as a thank you or a pay rise.

You must be honest at this stage. I know that the temptation, when you are unhappy, is to think that you never have your values met.

But the reality is that if you have been in your job for a long time, you are having some of your values met a lot of the time.

The next step is to identify what you can do to get your values met more often. For a start, you need to let people know what you want! If you want recognition, ask for feedback; do not wait for it to be offered.

SELLING

Many people believe that they cannot sell, whether they are thinking about selling themselves or selling a product or service. However, if you have ever persuaded your colleague to have a cream cake when they were on a diet, you can sell!

Some people find they have a mental block about the idea of selling because of what the word 'sales' means to them. What does it mean to you? Does it mean making people buy things they do not want? If you believe that, ask yourself how often you are persuaded to buy something that you really do not want? If you have really decided that you do not want something, nothing can persuade you otherwise.

If you look at selling as finding a solution to someone s problem or fulfilling their wants, it takes on an entirely different image.

The process of selling, from identifying potential customers, through information gathering to making the final offer allows you to match what you are offering to meet their needs.

Are you completely happy with what you are selling? Do you believe in it? Whether you are selling yourself or something else, you do need to believe that what you are selling is worthwhile in order for it, and you, to seem believable to your potential customers.

Think about ways to improve your self-image and your beliefs about the product or service.

If you are still worried about selling being about making someone buy something they do not want, remember the old saying; 'you can lead a horse to water, but you cannot make it drink'!

SERVICE
How frustrated to you feel when you get poor customer service? I was prompted to write this piece after spending two days at home, waiting for an engineer to turn up to repair my computer!

An important part of marketing is the customer service that is offered and provided. It is the experience that you take home with you as recall about how you are treated. It stays with you long after you have used the product or service.

So why is this relevant to you? Quite simply we are all service providers to our colleagues, subordinates and employers at work. The customer service you give to fellow workers is often the only tangible evidence that they have of the quality of your work. So being honest with yourself, do you give 100% excellent customer service 100% of the time?

Exceptional companies deliver customer service that is beyond their customers' expectations. **Do you do the same?**

When you bring your personal problems into work with you and allow your mood to be affected by them - service will suffer. How do you answer the telephone or greet people when they visit your desk? Do not allow your own bad day to make a day that is bad for others. Think of every person that you have contact with as a paying customer who expects and deserves good service.

So why does this matter? Well the benefits of providing better service means that you will stand out from the crowd and be far more likely to be considered for promotion because of the impression you have left with others. You will also have a great deal of pride in what you do and that is an excellent way of building your self-esteem.

Of course, as well as being a service provider, you are also a consumer who enjoys the benefits of good service from your suppliers. You will find that you will get as good as you give!

SUCCESS

If you do not know where you are going, how will you know when you have got there? Before starting out on any major change in your life, it is really important to set yourself an outcome. This trains your mind to start noticing the opportunities that arise to help you achieve it.

Define exactly what it is that you want to achieve. You must state it positively, for example, 'I want to get a new job,' rather than, 'I do not want to work here any more'. This will help you head towards what you want, a stronger motivator than moving away from what you do not want.

On any journey, it is important to know where you are going. Therefore, how will you know how and when you have achieved your outcome? When you have, how will things look? How will you feel? What great things will you be saying to congratulate yourself?

On a long car journey, you check road signs on the way to make sure you are going in the right direction. Do the same when you are planning how to achieve your outcomes. Set yourself goalposts for what you will have achieved in one month, three months, six months and a year s time (and longer if applicable).

Do something everyday towards achieving your outcome. Review your progress every month — if you find you are not making the effort to work towards your outcomes, it might be wise to find a coach to keep you on track.

STRESS

Have you heard the saying, **'Garbage in, Garbage out'**? In stress management terms, this means that you need to control what you are focusing on. Therefore, if you read newspapers, watch TV and listen to the radio news you will focus mainly on bad news. Most bad news is out of your control and this creates feelings of helplessness and stress. If you want to keep up-to-date with what is happening in the world, you only need to read one newspaper or watch or listen to the news once per day.

Similarly, soap operas and 'reality TV' shows focus on arguments and conflicts. If you watch many of these programmes, your body will respond as if the stress is happening to you and will create fight or flight chemical changes inside your body. Some research has proven raised blood pressure and cholesterol levels just from watching certain programmes!

Similarly, be aware of advertisements that aim to make you believe that your life will be perfect when you have bought the products. Think of the messages you are taking in when you look at them — you may feel a pleasure of desire and anticipation of buying, but you may become stressed because you start to worry how you can afford to buy it. It is useful to filter out any that you can define as 'wants' and limit purchases to your 'needs'.

To reduce the amount of stress in your life, you need to be aware of the stressful messages that daily bombard your subconscious. There is no need to shut yourself away from the world. There is a need to manage the information that you take in.

Choose television programmes that make you laugh. Read inspirational stories and watch or read the news only once a day. Listen to relaxing music. Learn to unwind.

SWOT

A popular technique with marketers is the SWOT analysis. This stands for analysing the organisation s Strengths, Weaknesses, Opportunities & Threats. It is used to help with planning future strategic moves. You too can use the technique to work out how you can market yourself further.

Your strengths and weaknesses are usually focused on you as an individual. For example, a strength could be that you are highly skilled at using computer software. A weakness could be that your knowledge of your industry or subject may be a bit rusty or out of date.

At the opposite end, opportunities and threats refer to outside factors that could become opportunities (such as a promotion becoming available in your company shortly) or threats (such as economic factors affecting the stability of your industry).

The reason for carrying out this audit is to identify and build on the strengths that you can promote to others, to work on any weaknesses to make yourself more marketable and identify any factors happening around you that you can take action to benefit from or avoid.

Your strengths are the things that you mention at interviews and performance appraisals when discussing promotions and pay reviews. Your weaknesses can be something that you choose to work on for your next year s objectives.

Any threats and opportunities can be used as guidance when you decide on your next career move.

TEAMS

Strong teams work well together because of a shared vision and mutual respect for each member. These conditions create trust and harmony in working relationships.

Whether you are the leader of the team or one of the members, you can contribute to its strength and effectiveness by examining the values and outcomes that are important, both to the team and to the individual members within the team.

Firstly, get together with your team members and brainstorm what you believe the company and team values are. If you are unsure, think about what is important in the way that the company works, how it interacts with other people and how it treats customers. Values are the guiding principles that govern how you operate. They do not change according to circumstances. Typical values may be integrity, truth and honesty.

Next, individually think about your own values in a work context. You have the opportunity to review any potential conflict between your own values and those of the team or company. Decide what has to change, or be changed, to satisfy all sets of values. The objective is that everyone in the team gets their individual values met whilst also meeting the team s objectives. The converse is that a conflict of values within the team will reduce its effectiveness.

You can use this technique to create more harmony in all your relationships by finding out what is important to the people you care about and then respecting those needs.

TELEPHONES

When you have a face to face conversation, you will both gain up to 80% of your understanding from facial expression, body language and breathing patterns.

When you have a telephone conversation, you can only use voice patterns to gain 100% of your understanding.

Imagine this. You feel a bit under the weather. Your boss has just reprimanded you about something trivial. The office joker is laughing loudly and distracting you. You are trying to resolve a difficult problem. Then your telephone rings. How will you answer and what message does your manner send to the other person? How do you think that will alter their perception of you as a person, your company and their understanding of the conversation?

How would you answer differently if everything in your world was absolutely perfect?

When you answer a telephone you may not know who is on the line. A poor telephone manner could lose a client, upset an innocent party or even lose you promotion! Find someone who has an answering machine and make a few calls to it. Then listen to the recording. Do you sound they way that you thought you sounded?

Whenever possible, stand up to answer your phone or, at very least sit erect. Smile because this will alter your tone and modulation. Be ready to write anything down. Believe that this could be one of the most important telephone calls you will ever receive and reply accordingly. Speak calmly and clearly.

Your caller has a reason for calling you. Respect their reasons and their time and speak as you would wish to be spoken to.

THANKS

There are some words that are simple, powerful and free. Unfortunately they all too frequently seem to be ignored.

You know how you feel when you have pulled out all the stops on a special project or task, you have given your all - and then some - you are exhausted by the effort. Then someone who matters and who you respect stops by and says, 'Thank You'. As long as they mean it, you feel good, you feel valued and you feel energised.

We all like to be thanked, but do you thank others often enough? Some bosses think that their staff do not deserve thanks for doing the job that they are paid to do. These bosses are wrong. Do not follow their ways. Whenever someone does something for you, take a few seconds to look them in the eye and say 'Thanks'.

If they have delivered excellence, you may even like to add something tangible but of small cash value. For example, a suitable card will be displayed with pride and then taken home where it will be shown off again.

A close relative of thanks, is please. Whenever you ask someone to do something, unless it is an absolute order in circumstances of urgency, remember to say 'please'. It may seem like old fashioned courtesy, but it can make a big difference to the way that the job is accepted and executed.

Little words mean a lot. 'Thanks' and 'please' can make your life easier, allow you to establish rapport and to earn respect.

THOUGHTS

Ralph Waldo Emerson, the great American Philosopher, wrote; A man is what he thinks all day long. Your thoughts affect your emotions and your beliefs about yourself. If you change one of these 3 things, because of the link between them the rest will change too. It is quicker and more powerful to change your beliefs because these are your rules for how you judge your satisfaction with your life.

Firstly, make a list of everything that you believe about yourself in relation to your career. Split this list into positive beliefs about yourself and negative, limiting beliefs about yourself.

Take each limiting belief you have identified one by one and answer the following questions about it:

How is this belief ridiculous? Who did I pick it up from? Do I still respect this person in this aspect as I once did? What does this belief cost me on a daily basis? What will the long-term cost be, if I don t let go of this belief?

The next part of the exercise is to create an opposing positive empowering belief for every limiting belief you have written down.

Finally, for the next two weeks when you are reading newspapers, magazines and books and watching TV, look for evidence to prove your new empowering beliefs, for example, look for stories and examples of other people who are following your empowering beliefs. This will start to give you proof to support your new beliefs.

With any new task or project that you undertake, always ask yourself what you would need to believe in order to succeed with it — if you believe you can do anything you want you will find that you will be much more likely to be successful.

TIME

There are only so many hours in the day and it is said that you cannot manage time, you can only manage yourself. So, why are some people good at time management while others struggle to meet deadlines and get work finished?

Firstly, decide upon your objectives, both at work and at home. If you are clear on these, you will be better able to prioritise your tasks. Remember to describe each objective in terms of a tangible result.

Steven Covey, author of The Seven Habits of Highly Effective People, recommends that you split a page into 4 quarters and mark each of the quarters as follows; 'urgent and important', 'not urgent but important', 'urgent and not important' and 'not urgent and not important'. Then allocate all your tasks into the appropriate box. For example, leaving work on time to see your kids in their school play would be 'not urgent but important'.

As you use this model, eliminate as many tasks as possible from the quarters marked 'urgent and not important' and 'not urgent and not important'. These will be things that usually meet other people s objectives but not your own. Think about what you can delegate or negotiate from these quarters to give you more time to spend on the tasks in the important quarters.

Then prioritise what is left and work through them. It is human nature to do the easy tasks first. Do not be tempted. Get the difficult ones out of the way, then you can enjoy the rest of your day.

TIME OUT
Try these questions for size. Do you feel stress if you take time off work? How many holidays have you interrupted or cancelled during your career? Do you keep in touch with work when you are away?

You are not alone! Recent research has shown that fewer employees take their full holiday entitlement each year. Your time out is an important component of your total employment package. If you have chosen self employment it is equally important to plan for adequate breaks.

Perhaps you stay at work because you have important projects or feel that you are the only person who can handle something. These and similar excuses may mask the true reasons why you feel uncomfortable about taking your full vacation entitlement. The true causes need to be identified so that you can enjoy the recuperative benefits of a break.

Do you feel that your colleagues will realise that they can do without you? This reveals a basic doubt about your security that you should address. Do you lack trust in others to do a job or project as well as you could do it yourself? Ask why you lack this trust and what it might say about your delegation abilities. Are you afraid that something sinister may be discovered about you in your absence?

All of these examples are rooted in fear. When you are excellent at what you do, and when you do what you have to do with excellence, you have nothing to fear.

Planned maintenance programmes acknowledge the fact that machinery needs regular maintenance or repair if it is to function correctly with optimum productivity. You are more complex and sensitive than any machine. You need regular periods of relaxation to recharge your batteries, to stimulate your creativity and to recover from fatigue.

Even if you love your job, when you fail to take your holiday entitlement it is the equivalent of handing part of your salary back to your employer. You may also send the message that you think their allowance is too generous and that could backfire on your colleagues too. You must use it or you could lose it in more ways than one!

TRACKING

Take time out regularly to track your career progress. Find your diary and set aside one day in Spring, Summer, Autumn and Winter to review your job satisfaction levels. Do not wait for that first date to arrive, but start right now.

Begin by listing everything that is important to you in your work or career. Never mind the colour of the walls or the shape of your desk or bench. Instead, focus on matters like creativity, responsibility, respect and trust. Continue with this list until you have at least ten words on it or, until you simply run out of ideas.

This is a list of the values that are important to you. Now take each item in turn and ask yourself, 'How satisfied am I with this value?' Write your score out of ten by each one - where ten means 'highly satisfied' and one means 'highly dissatisfied'.

Take a few minutes to think about how you will feel when you have a perfect '10' against each value. This is similar to the way that sports competitors prepare mentally to exceed their previous best result. By imagining what they want and then rehearsing the feelings that will result from the perfect jump, throw, race or swim - they prepare their mind and body to recognise perfection and to achieve it.

To get on track, examine each value that has a score below ten. Then, write down three actions that you could take to raise your scores. Remember to include a date for taking each step. For example you might define, 'Make an appointment today to discuss my progress with the boss'.

This simple exercise may reveal some surprising truths. It will certainly help you to keep on a track that is in accordance with your personal values and that will result in greater job satisfaction and happiness.

TRICKS

Elsewhere we discussed acting 'as if' in order to create confident feelings. One way to always be able to 'act as if' is to have beliefs about yourself such as 'I am good at '. If you believe that you are good at something, you will automatically feel confident when doing it.

We often think we are not confident about anything in life, but we forget the areas of our lives where we are confident and only focus on what we are lacking. Think about all the things you do in a day, for example getting out of bed, getting dressed, walking, talking, cooking, driving, playing sport. We take any of those things for granted, but there was a time when all those things were new to us and we were not sure we would ever master them.

It is the same with the areas of your life where you currently feel less confident. One day they will just become one of those everyday things that you do. Our creator had a sense of humour when he made us — he wanted us to grow and stretch ourselves constantly. All things in nature must grow and adapt to their environment, otherwise they become extinct. So, if you accept that you will always be learning new things, doubting your ability will always be a necessary step in the process. It is a sign of growth. It is better to be green and growing rather than ripe and rotten!

UNCERTAINTY

We are living in changing times; the media is full of stories of possible recession and job losses. There are ways to reduce the feelings of loss, of being out of control and uncertainty.

Think about when you decided to leave a job — it feels completely different from when the job leaves you. This is because you make the decision and are in control. Therefore, by reframing to the positive things about a potential change you can take back any control that you feel is missing.

Firstly, talk to your boss. Find out as much as you can and how the company changes will affect you. Act in a professional manner with them, confirming your commitment to the job but reminding them that you need information to plan your future.

If the company is offering you a redundancy package that includes a lump sum payment, think about what you want to do with it. Will you use it to boost your savings, pay off a mortgage, pay for you to retrain or travel, take an extended break from work, start your own business?

Update your CV and start being alert for potential opportunities. Read the careers section of your local newspapers and the trade press relevant to your industry. Talk to recruitment agencies. Apply for jobs to gain interview practice. This is particularly useful if you have worked for your current employer for many years and have not attended an interview for some time.

VALUES

An organisation has a set of values that have been derived from the behaviour of the directors and has cascaded down through the organisation.

For example, the values of a chairman or managing director may include the need to be competitive and make money. Individuals further down the hierarchy, who do not share the same values, will be uncomfortable within this environment, will not achieve their targets and may end up leaving the company.

This is caused by a conflict of values. We often think that opposites attract. However, there have to be many similarities to render the differences unimportant. So, if you are finding that you are unhappy at work, it could be because there is a conflict between your values and the organisation s.

To identify your values, write down everything that is important to you in a work context. For example, FREEDOM may be important to you. Keep writing until you have a list of at least 10 words like this in it. Looking at your list, how do you feel it compares with how you are treated at work? If you are given a list of rules that you must obey, you may feel a little stifled by it!

If you identify major differences between your values and those of your organisation, you need to find ways to negotiate so that both you and your employer are happy. Or, if you cannot stand the heat, seek a cooler kitchen to work in!

WIN-WIN

When you are queuing for something, you do not care about anyone else as long as you get what you want. In this negotiation, when you win the person further down the line loses. However, when you are involved in negotiations within long-term relationships, such as with your boss or colleagues, there are times when only win-win will do.

This is not about compromising. It happens when you and the other party come up with a solution together that is better than your original separate solutions.

So, how do you manage negotiations to improve your chances of achieving a win-win situation? This technique is excellent to use, particularly if emotions are high or if parties do not understand each other.

Firstly, you must agree on what you both want at the top level. For example, you may agree that you both want a successful outcome to the meeting. It is good to get this objective agreed at the start so that, if you disagree in the detail later, you can keep it in mind.

Next comes the hard part! Each party must let the other speak in turn without interruption or defence. When one party is speaking, the other must give full attention and must check that they understand by repeating back what they have heard. This goes a very long way to creating a feeling of trust and understanding. However, it isn t easy and needs practice!

Finally, once you have both had your say, think win-win and come up with much better alternatives than you both first thought of.

DISCOVER COACHING

If you are responsible for managing others — whether at work or at home — it can be quite exhausting. One way to relieve your burden of people management is to adopt a coaching approach to your style of leadership.

What is coaching? Coaching is a practice that successful managers and leaders do to help their staff develop independently. Coaching encourages people to get clarity about what they want to achieve, to take responsibility for their success and be motivated to take action. Coaching is NOT about a manager giving advice or providing the answers or instructions for staff to go away and follow.

Who uses coaching? Coaching is being used widely within organisations and with individuals who want to take control of their future. Those people who want to set goals and guarantee their achievement.

How would coaching help you as a manager or leader? Coaching gives others the power to be more independent and builds their confidence so that you develop a stronger team. There is less emotional exhaustion for you, as you will find you do not have to keep motivating others. Through coaching, they will find their own motivation.

How do you become a coach? There are some fundamental differences between a coach and a manager. Instead of telling, a coach asks many questions then actively listens to the answers. A coach never seeks to judge, only to understand. A coach believes that everyone has the answers within themselves.

It can be a challenge to give up old behaviour if you are used to controlling other s actions, but the benefits will be worth much more than the cost of changing your style of managing.

THE CREDITS

THE AUTHOR
Sarah Urquhart is a Career and Executive Coach. She is also a management trainer and a horse behaviouralist. You can contact her at sarah@thecoachingclinic.com

THE PUBLISHER
The Coaching Academy is Europe's premier coach training school. For their information brochure about coaching call 0800 783 4823

THE EDITOR
Colin Edwards is a professional freelance editor with a coaching background.